WILLIAM AND CATHERINE
BOOTH

Founders of The Salvation Army

Helen K. Hosier

BARBOUR
PUBLISHING, INC.
Uhrichsville, Ohio

ooks in the "Heroes of the Faith" series:

Gladys Aylward
John Bunyan
William Carey
Amy Carmichael
George Washington Carver
Fanny Crosby
Jim Elliot
Charles Finney
Billy Graham
C. S. Lewis
David Livingstone
Martin Luther

D. L. Moody
Samuel Morris
George Müller
Watchman Nee
John Newton
Mary Slessor
Charles Spurgeon
Corrie ten Boom
Mother Teresa
Sojourner Truth
John Wesley

ISBN 1-57748-505-X

Unless otherwise noted, Scripture quotations are taken from the Authorized King James Version of the Bible.

Scripture quotations marked (NKJV) are taken from the New King James Version. Copyright © 1979, 1980, 1982 by Thomas Nelson, Inc. Used by permission. All rights reserved.

Published by Barbour Publishing, Inc., P.O. Box 719, Uhrichsville, OH 44683 http://www.barbourbooks.com

ecpa Member of the
Evangelical Christian
Publishers Association

Published in the United States of America.

WILLIAM AND CATHERINE
BOOTH

one

"No, never!"

Every head turned; all eyes were fixed on the speaker in the gallery. It was a woman's voice, which made the words even more shocking.

In the spring of 1861, the annual meeting of the Methodist New Connexion was no place for a woman to speak her mind, but Catherine Booth could not restrain herself. She felt betrayed by the man who had drawn both her and her husband, William, into the reform-oriented denomination seven years before.

In 1854, the Reverend Dr. William Cooke had seen great potential in William and had encouraged the Booths to become part of the New Connexion work in London. Here, he assured them, was a place where Christians would be taught to honor Christ by letting their faith affect the everyday details of their lives.

Now this same man was interfering with their dreams

for revival meetings all across England. And he called it a compromise! Catherine saw it as a compromise with pious mediocrity and petty jealousy.

William had proven himself to be a very effective preacher, but for the past five years, Catherine had watched as opposition to him grew among some leaders in the denomination. It began when, after a series of meetings William held in Nottingham, P. J. Wright, the superintendent of the circuit, began to oppose his work. This was a serious development because the circuit system was the basis for the New Connexion's entire organizational framework.

Each circuit consisted of several groups of believers who lived within a single geographic area. Some groups had only a few members and met in a private home, while others were large enough to need their own church building. The members of each group prayed, studied, and worshiped together. They also held each other accountable for the spiritual quality of their daily lives. They were assisted by one or more ministers. If one circuit objected to William's methods, others might follow suit. Then where would he be able to preach?

William's evangelistic meetings were aggressively publicized in a society where holiness was usually associated with polite, sedate, private behavior. Lists of those who needed salvation or a renewed commitment to Christ were developed, and these people were prayed for by name in public meetings before the revival services began. Some of the people on these lists were civic leaders, successful businesspeople, or even prominent members of local churches. For them to be identified as "sinners" was considered embarrassing, insulting, and perhaps slanderous.

Those who attended William's meetings were asked to make an immediate public commitment to Christ by coming forward and kneeling in front of all those in attendance. The meetings sometimes became very long as several appeals for a response were made. As the meetings grew longer, they often became very emotional, and this led to charges that people were being forced into irresponsible decisions for Christ, rather than being encouraged to make thoughtful and carefully considered ones. It was assumed by some leaders within the New Connexion that people who were coerced into following Christ would soon turn their backs on that decision.

During the meetings and the work that was done with new converts afterward, laypeople—both men and women —were assigned important duties that had formerly been performed only by ordained ministers.

The participation of women in the meetings was particularly controversial. Many Christian leaders believed that the Bible commanded women to keep silent in church or be carefully and constantly submissive to every man around them. It did not help the Booths' situation that Catherine had been a strong advocate for the unlimited involvement of women in all aspects of worship, teaching, and leadership in the church since before she married William.

Whatever the exact cause of Wright's opposition to William's preaching methods, it is clear that much of the problem was a simple matter of jealousy. William was such a dynamic speaker and drew such large crowds that he made most of the other pastors in the New Connexion look very inadequate by comparison.

William and Catherine were committed to their approach to ministry, however, and served in several communities, including Gateshead, a town of fifty thousand, located just across the river Tyne from Newcastle, on the northeastern coast of England. By the summer of 1860, William had become quite ill. The combined pressures of pastoral duties and evangelistic endeavors were partly to blame. The stubborn unwillingness of New Connexion leaders to assign him to full-time evangelism added more stress. The attacks on Catherine because of her work at Gateshead and her outspoken advocacy for women in the church also weighed heavily on him. It took months for William to recover his health. During that time, Catherine took over virtually all of his duties.[1]

Soon, her remarkable abilities were clear to all, and her fame as "the woman preacher" was spreading far beyond Gateshead. But this was a time when most Victorian women wore gloves, carried delicate fans, and kept their pretty mouths shut, at least in public. Catherine's strong opinions and great success as a preacher combined with William's uniquely powerful ministry soon had many leaders in the New Connexion whispering, "These independent Booths need curbing."

In December 1860, William returned to his work at Gateshead, and on Christmas Day, he and Catherine shared the preaching duties at Bethesda Chapel.[2]

During the first few months of 1861, Catherine began to regularly accept invitations to preach in public—and not just as a replacement for her ailing husband. The last restraints on her role in their shared ministry were cast aside.

On March 5, 1861, William wrote a lengthy letter to the Reverend James Stacey, the retiring president of the New Connexion, pressing for reassignment to evangelism full-time.[3] The detailed plan showed how William's itinerant work could be supported by the denomination and would enhance their outreach efforts.

Catherine had grown very frustrated with New Connexion Methodism and was urging her husband to consider an independent ministry of some kind. But she was also willing to stay at Gateshead, so long as "the Lord's leading" was their first priority.[4] She also had some anxious thoughts about the future. She was now the mother of four young children. They had a good home and a settled income, but only so long as they remained at Gateshead. The membership of Bethesda Chapel had grown dramatically and the Sunday services were crowded, but Catherine was concerned about her husband's health, as well as her own.

Larger family issues also troubled her. She worried about her parents, who lived far away in London. Her father was prone to wild swings of emotion and had struggled in the past with alcoholism. Then there was William's widowed mother, who still looked to her son for support.

As the New Connexion's annual conference convened in Liverpool that May, it was clear to William and Catherine that they had reached a turning point in their lives. They knew their own future would be one of the most hotly debated topics at the conference. With the work at Gateshead prospering, no one disputed how much the whole denomination benefitted from the Booths' ministry. As the conference began, William was ready to risk everything by forcing the issue of his assignment to full-time evangelistic work. "I'll try again," he told Catherine. "I'll make a strong plea for them to allow me to do the itinerant evangelism work and relinquish the circuit pastoral duties."

"I'll be in the gallery praying for you," she assured him.

All during the week, William waited for an opportunity to be heard. Finally, on Saturday, May 25, the question of the Booths' future was at last raised. It had already been a long week and the attendees were tired and fidgety. William's proposal was presented by the Reverend J. Stokoe and carefully considered arguments were given in favor of it.

Then P. J. Wright and his supporters brought arguments against the proposal. The battle began. Frustrated voices were raised on both sides of the argument, but it was clear that many at the meeting were deeply angry with both of the Booths for their unwillingness to submit to the guidance of denominational leaders.

"His request is against all reason and authority," one minister stated flatly.

Another critic suggested that William's popularity was damaging the whole circuit system. His revival meetings could easily add hundreds of new converts to a circuit, but neither he nor his wife were interested in staying in the area to help care for them. Worse still, many of the new believers were disappointed by the stale traditionalism of the established churches. They were more interested in going to the next series of revival meetings in a nearby town than in working to build up the local circuit.

"He is taking the cream and leaving the skimmed milk for others," the man loudly complained.

As time passed, the discussion grew even more heated. Some argued that it was an insult to any pastor to bring in someone from the outside to conduct evangelistic services. Others vehemently denounced the emotional excesses of all revivalism. Speaker after speaker acknowledged that William possessed exceptional gifts but then went on to stubbornly argue that these gifts could be best used within a single circuit.

One speaker pointed to William's long illness during the preceding year and suggested that all the travel was "bad for him; bad for the circuit."

With the meeting rapidly deteriorating into an abusive shouting match between supporters and opponents of William and Catherine, Dr. Henry Crofts, president of the New Connexion, stopped the proceedings. Then he requested that the gallery be cleared so the discussion could take place "with closed doors."

All during the rancorous debate, Catherine and William had been exchanging glances—he from the conference floor below, she from the upper gallery. As Catherine stood to leave, she was overcome with disappointment and indignation at what she had heard and seen. At first she was carried slowly along by the press of people around her. She approached the outer hall and the stairs down to the main level of the hall.

She hesitated, lingering at the door to the stairs. She

couldn't bring herself to abandon William at such a crucial moment. A thought suddenly struck her: *He will look up for my support, and I won't be there*. Instead of leaving, she remained at the head of the stairs where she could still hear the proceedings. She could also still see much of the floor below, but those below could not easily see her.

William was given an opportunity to read his March letter to the Reverend James Stacey, but even his eloquence did not settle the issue.

Hoping to salvage something for the Connexion and for William, Dr. Cooke, his old mentor, proposed a compromise amendment. "If Booth takes over the Newcastle circuit, couldn't he, by special arrangement with his officers, occasionally take time out for evangelistic work elsewhere?" He went on to suggest that William concentrate on his duties as a pastor, limit his evangelistic work, and refrain from holding revival meetings in other circuits without the consent of the ministers who oversaw them.

William's heart sank within him as the amendment was quickly passed by a large majority. All this had been tried before, and all of it had failed!

Suddenly, Catherine's frustration at the formalities of the conference, and her anger at the spiritual blindness of those who opposed her husband's mission to evangelize England could no longer be contained. "No, never!" she loudly exclaimed.

As William sat quietly, his chin resting on his left hand, his right arm crossed in front of him, he heard Catherine's clear voice ringing out from above.

Bewilderment, dismay, and outrage registered on the

faces around him. "Are the doors not closed?" cried Dr. Crofts. "Close the doors!"

Catherine quickly found herself taken firmly by the arm and ushered down the stairs. William quietly took up his hat and walked to the rear door of the hall. There he met Catherine and embraced her fiercely. Together they left the building.

Behind them, the hall erupted into chaos, while several voices shouted, "Order! Order!"

Strange as it may seem, William and Catherine were not quite done with the New Connexion. They yielded to an offer from Dr. Cooke to make William the superintendent of Newcastle circuit, one of the most important in the denomination.

But the die had been set. Although no one expected it, before long the Booths would begin a journey that would lead to the founding of one of the great Christian organizations of the nineteenth and twentieth centuries. But then few would have expected the widow's son to have entered the ministry in the first place.

two

On April 10, 1829, the piercing wail of a newborn baby broke out at 12 Nottintone Place, Sneinton, a suburb of Nottingham. William Booth had just made his entrance into the world. The Booth family lived in a six-room house made of red brick. William's mother, Mary, was Samuel Booth's second wife, and they shared their small space with William's sisters, Ann, Mary, and Emma.

The Booths kept to themselves. William's mother had grown up with an aunt and uncle in a rural cottage after her own mother died. She'd never been outgoing. She and her husband didn't enjoy socializing. One family friend described the Booths as "proud and reserved." But the Booths were quite strict about making sure their children attended church every week.

William's father was a builder. At times he made a good living, and he planned on making his only son a gentleman, which in British society would give him prestige and easier access to good jobs. William was told that he would attend Mr. Biddulph's school to get the education and friendships needed to become a British gentleman.

Unfortunately, hard times had hit Nottingham and the surrounding villages. Because people were losing their jobs, William's father couldn't sell or rent the homes he was building. Without money to pay the bills he owed, Samuel Booth lost the houses he had built one by one. Eventually the Booths lost the mortgage on their own house.

There was no money to pay for William to continue going to school. In fact, the family had difficulty keeping food on the table. So rather than training to be a gentleman, thirteen-year-old William was apprenticed to a pawnbroker, Francis Eames, who lived and worked in Nottingham's Goose Gate section. Goose Gate was a horrible section of the city. People lived on the streets because they couldn't afford to rent even a small room. They struggled to find food to eat and clothes to wear.

While William's master, Mr. Eames, provided him with food and a place to sleep, he also worked William hard. Like most apprentices in his day, William received little pay for work that lasted from early morning to late evening. Instead of being paid well, he was supposed to be learning a business that would supply him with an income for life once he completed his apprenticeship.

William had been working for Mr. Eames for less than a year when he received word that his father, Samuel Booth, had died. "I had scarcely an income as an apprentice," William remembered, "and was so hard up when my father died, that I could do next to nothing to assist my dear mother and sisters, which was the cause of no little humiliation and grief."[1]

But William had no other options. Until he was nineteen years old, he was obligated to work for Mr. Eames. Apprentices signed contracts with their masters which gave the masters total control over their lives for six or seven years. Those contracts didn't allow the apprentices to leave if they didn't like the situation. Runaway apprentices couldn't get other jobs and were doomed to a life of poverty. So fourteen-year-old William kept working for Mr. Eames and sent home what little money he could to help his mother and sisters.

Obviously William's pay wasn't enough to support the entire family, so his mother took a job running a small shop in Goose Gate as well. She sold household wares to her customers. Between William's apprentice salary and his mother's earnings at the shop, they were able to keep their family together.

During these hard times, William's mother counseled him, "Be good, William, and all will be well." When William wrote about his youth, he left the impression that his mother was a strong Christian influence. He spoke very lovingly of her, praising her for what she had done for him and his sisters.

But at the time, William was more influenced by his friends. He wrote that his companions' "influence was anything but beneficial" and reported that, "I went down hill morally, and the consequences might have been serious."[2]

William's work as a pawnbroker's apprentice gave

him firsthand opportunities to see the misery of the city's poor. He saw the desperation in people's eyes as they brought wedding rings, Sunday silk handkerchiefs, umbrellas, and printed shawls to the pawnshop. By exchanging their few belongings for cash, they hoped simply to stay alive and avoid eviction from their homes. Because the pawnbroker resold their belongings at a much higher price than he bought them for, few sellers were ever able to buy back their treasures.

Memories of children crying for bread on the streets of Nottingham stayed with William throughout his long life. One evening he saw ragged men and women smash windows to get into a bakery. Seconds later, they fled, their arms crammed with loaves of bread. William learned a lesson about how hunger led people to take desperate actions.

Between his friendships and his work, William might eventually have become just one more person exploiting poor people in their desperation. But a year after his father died, something happened that changed the direction of William's life. At fifteen years of age, William Booth began attending the Broad Street Wesleyan Chapel, part of the Wesleyan Methodist Church.

During services, William became increasingly aware of his own sinfulness. The lay preacher Isaac Marsden stirred the teenage boy's heart by warning that souls die every minute. William could not recall the exact moment of his conversion—it may have been at a prayer meeting or it may have been in private—but he often recounted in vivid detail the night in 1844 when he was trudging home from a meeting on unpaved streets. Suddenly a sense of spiritual exaltation flooded through his whole being. While the experience may not have been as dramatic as the New Testament account of Saul of Tarsus being blinded by a brilliant light on the Damascus Road, it was nonetheless real. William stood on the darkened street and knew he must renounce sin and take care of wrongs he'd done to others.

The first thing he did after this experience was to gather a group of friends who had given him a silver pencil case in recognition of a favor they thought he had done for them. In reality, William hadn't done the favor they credited to him. He knew he had to make things right with these friends if he was serious about obeying Jesus, but it was not easy for him to do. He wrote, "Merely to return their gift would have been comparatively easy, but to confess the deception I had practised upon them was a humiliation to which for some days I could not bring myself."

After days of internal struggle, William Booth finally determined that he must make things right. Later he wrote, "I remember, as if it were but yesterday, . . .the finding of the young fellow I had chiefly wronged, the acknowledgment of my sin, the return of the pencil-case—the instant rolling away from my heart of the guilty burden, the peace that came in its place, and the going forth to serve my God and my generation from that hour."[3]

Because of his contract, William continued to work for Mr. Eames in the pawnshop. But he understood that he had to change how he was using his free time or he would not be able to serve God. Increasingly he spent every free moment in church and ministering to other people. "God shall have all there is of William Booth," he declared.

By the time he was seventeen, William was trying to follow in the footsteps of an American revivalist, James Caughey, whom he had seen hold revivals in Nottingham during 1846. William and his friend Will Sansom set out for the impoverished Meadow Platts neighborhood. According to Booth, "We used to take out a chair into the street, and one of us mounting it would give out a hymn, which we then sang with the help of, at the most, three or four people. Then I would talk to the people, and invite them to come with us to a meeting in one of the houses."[4] Lively songs and short messages led to conversions.

Young William Booth and his friend were not satisfied with simply holding meetings. They wanted to help God change people's lives. So they visited the sick and the converts whose names and addresses they had recorded. Often he didn't get home until midnight, and he didn't get as much sleep as he needed because he had to be at Mr. Eames's shop, ready to work, by 7:00 every morning. William acknowledged later that this schedule wore down his health, but he also learned through both the work he did and the mistakes he made. Much later, he wrote about those early efforts, "We had a miniature Salvation Army."

As their ministry continued, William Booth and Will Sansom became even closer friends. Booth compared their friendship to that of David and Jonathan in the Bible. But tragedy was all too near. Will Sansom suddenly became very ill, probably with tuberculosis. His family took him to the country, hoping the cleaner air and rest would heal his body. But nothing worked. Eventually they took Will to the Isle of Wight, hoping that the moist sea air would be easier for him to breathe. In spite of all their efforts, young Will Sansom died.

William Booth was devastated. His coworker who had been so essential to the work they were doing among the poor was gone. To make matters worse, William was convinced that his work at the pawnshop was interfering with his ability to keep Sunday as a day of rest. Because the pawnshop was particularly busy on Saturday nights, Mr. Eames frequently had his entire staff work well past midnight. William Booth believed his day of rest should begin immediately after midnight on Saturday. When William shared his concerns with his relatives and Christian friends, many of them thought he was being overly conscientious. But William was determined to follow his conscience.

He asked to speak with Mr. Eames. During the meeting, William explained, "I am willing to begin on Monday morning as soon as the clock strikes twelve and work until the clock strikes twelve on Saturday night, but not one hour or one minute of Sunday will I work for you or all your money."

Mr. Eames responded, "You'll work with the rest of us until we shut up the shop." When he observed William's reaction, he added, "Or you can leave." The weekend drew near. Everyone wondered what William would do. On Saturday morning, William arrived for work as scheduled. But when the pawnshop stayed open after midnight, William quietly got up and left. True to his word, Mr.

Eames fired him. Because Mr. Eames provided his apprentices with a place to sleep, William was now both jobless and homeless. Later, he said that "I was laughed at by everybody as a sort of fool."

In spite of the difficulties, William held to his beliefs. Within a week, Mr. Eames had a change of heart. The pawnbroker realized he'd lost one of his most valuable employees and that having an apprentice with so much integrity could be good for business. Mr. Eames offered William his job back and promised him that he could finish work at the stroke of midnight on Saturday. When a couple weeks later, Mr. Eames got married and took his bride on a honeymoon trip to Paris, he left William in charge of the shop.[5]

The death of Will Sansom left William even more determined to minister to the poor people of Nottingham. After work, he carried the war against sin and misery into the open air in Red Lion Square or down in "The Bottoms," one of Nottingham's cruelest neighborhoods. He earned the nickname "Wilful Will" from Nottingham's citizens for his fiery and passionate concern for the lost. It was common for revivalists to visit the English chapels during what was called "The Hungry Forties." Whenever they appeared, William attended every meeting, absorbing whatever he could from these older men.

Borrowing the speaking techniques of these more experienced evangelists, William would seek out groups of men who were drinking or hanging out. His powerful voice cut like a whip as he said: "I want to put a few straight questions to your souls. Have any of *you* got a child at home without shoes to its feet? Are *your* wives sitting now in dark houses awaiting for you to return without money? Are you going away from here. . .*to spend on drink money that your wives need for food?"*

Booth was also convinced that the wealthiest in Nottingham should show God's love to the neediest street person. One Sunday, the Reverend Samuel Dunn was sitting comfortably on his ornate red plush pulpit chair in the Broad Street Chapel and the congregation was singing, when the chapel's outer door suddenly swung open. In came a shuffling, shabby, almost ragged contingent of men and women, obviously nervous and uncomfortable in the presence of the chapel people who were made up mostly of mill managers, shopkeepers, and their well-dressed wives.

Behind the ragged group stood "Wilful Will," blocking the efforts of those visitors who were fearful and wanting to leave the church. Then William began ushering his charges into the pews. The Reverend Dunn watched in dismay. It was totally unprecedented. In those days, the poor, if they even came to chapel, entered by another door and were segregated onto benches with no backs or cushions, behind a partition which screened them from the eyes of the congregation, as well as the pulpit. The regular members of the congregation stared, glared, whispered, and snorted. Some changed seats to avoid any contact with the "riff-raff."

Following the service, young William Booth was confronted by angry deacons and the pastor. "Now, lad," the Reverend Dunn began, "it's a fine thing you are doing to help these poor souls, but you should have sat them in the reserved section. In the future, if you wish to bring in such people, they are to enter by the side door and sit on those benches."

"I don't see why," young William said. "They came to worship God the same as the rest of us. Are they to be set apart for that?"

"No, no, lad, of course not. But—well, William, they may be crawling with lice and vermin, and they make our good women uneasy."

"They did the best they could with what they have. They've cleaned themselves up for this occasion. I know their clothes are shabby and threadbare, but I'm not interested in their clothes. I'm interested in their souls."

"Well, uh. . .that's another thing. . .walking in the front door looking like that gives decent people the wrong impression about our congregation," responded one churchman. Glancing around for support from the others, he continued, "We must insist that if you bring this rabble here again, you bring them in through the back door and seat them in the poor section."

"They're not rabble," Booth said. "They're men and women seeking salvation—and it seems to me that in the house of God they should be free to sit where they please. Good day, gentlemen."

It was his first brush with church society, but the memory of that event burned itself into his heart and mind and was to become a determining force in the years ahead. His actions made many of the people in his church indignant. Even his own mother and sisters believed that salvation for these drunken outcasts was not possible. They may have been sincere in their beliefs, but they were wrong and the young man knew it.

The Reverend Dunn, however, observed that William was having incredible results in his street preaching and suggested to him that he consider going "on the plan" as a local preacher to villages. "Going on the plan" was the first step into Wesleyan Methodist ministry. Men on the plan preached when an ordained minister was unavailable. At first William declined the invitation, but then he changed his mind and became an accredited, unpaid local preacher.

At about this time, William's pawnbroking apprenticeship ended, and he couldn't find work. He was nineteen years old. Thirteen-hour workdays for six years, the bad air in the pawnshop, lack of regular sleep, and unhealthy eating habits had taken their toll. Nagging, uncomfortable indigestion was an ever-present torment. The doctor warned him that a man with a nervous system like his needed a frame like a bullock and a chest like a prizefighter to survive.

William was further discouraged because the members of his church didn't seem concerned about his well-being. Of that low time in his life he wrote that "no one took the slightest interest in me."

Aware that he needed to conserve his energies and regain his health if he hoped to be used in the Lord's work, William concentrated on getting well. Because he didn't have a job, he spent his time studying and reading. In particular he read Charles Finney's *Lectures on Revivals of Religion* and sermons and books by George Whitefield and John Wesley.

In describing his early love of Methodism, William wrote: "I worshiped everything that bore the name of Methodist. . . . I had devoured the story of [John

Wesley's] life. No human compositions seemed to me to be comparable to his writings, and to the hymns of his brother Charles; and all that was wanted, in my estimation, for the salvation of the world was the faithful carrying into practice of the letter and spirit of his instructions.

"I cared little then or afterwards for ecclesiastical creeds or forms. What I wanted to see was an organization with the salvation of the world as its supreme ambition and object, worked upon the simple, earnest principles which I had myself embraced, and which, youth as I was, I had already seen carried into successful practice."

In spite of his enthusiasm for studying, William realized he couldn't stay unemployed forever. His mother and sisters still needed financial support. Having recovered some of his health, William considered his options. While he was a lay preacher, he quickly dismissed the idea of pursuing ordination. It cost money to prepare for preaching—money that wasn't available. There was only one vocation open to him: the pawnbroking trade.

William quickly realized the only place he'd be able to find such work was in London. His move to the Walworth section of that great city was the last thing he wanted to do. But with the responsibility for his mother and sisters' care, how could he turn down a job offer which included a room above the shop as well as meals?

With mixed feelings, William Booth made his way to London. In some ways, he found life in London worse than he had imagined. His new job was not pleasant. Later he described himself as being "practically a white slave." But William saw his job as a way to provide for his family's financial needs. The work he cared about most was the volunteer work he did after the pawnshop closed.

Soon after his move to London, William became associated with Walworth Chapel. The congregation gave him many opportunities for lay preaching on Sundays. Sometimes he was sent to churches as far away as Greenwich, eight miles south of the city. William was tall and gaunt, and after a long day of preaching, his weary legs pounded the pavement to reach his dismal room before 10:00 when the owner locked the doors.

He maintained contact with his friends in Nottingham through letters. In one such letter he described what kept him going during those lonely days in London: "How are you going on? I know you are living to God, and working for Jesus. Grasp still firmer the standard! Unfold still wider the battle-flag! Press still closer on the ranks of the enemy, and mark your pathway still more distinctly with glorious trophies of Emmanuel's grace, and with enduring monuments of Jesus' power! The trumpet has given the signal for the conflict! Your General assures you of success and a glorious reward, your crown is already held out. Then why delay? Why doubt? Onward! Onward! Onward! Christ for me! Be that your motto; be that your battle-cry; be that your war-note; be that your consolation; be that your plea when asking mercy of God; your end when offering it to man; your hope when encircled by darkness; your triumph and victory when attacked and overcome by death! Christ for me! Tell it to men who are living and dying in sin! Tell it to Jesus, that you have chosen Him to be your Saviour and your God; tell it to devils, and bid them cease to harass, since you are determined to die for the truth!"

In closing that letter, William spoke of the difficulties he was encountering in ministry: "I preached on Sabbath last—a respectable but dull and lifeless congregation. Notwithstanding, I had liberty both praying and preaching. I had not the assistance of a single 'Amen' or 'Hallelujah' the whole of the service! It is hard work to labour for an hour and a half in the pulpit, and then come down and have to do the work of the prayer meeting as well!"

His letter then issued a plea to his friends to involve themselves in lay preaching: "I want some Savages and Proctors and Frosts and Hoveys and Robinsons here with me in the prayer meetings, and, glory to God, we would carry all before us! Praise God for living at Nottingham every hour you are in it! Oh, to live to Christ on earth, and to meet you once more, never to part, in a better world!"[6]

Many years later when collecting information about his life and recording his memories for the year 1850, William Booth wrote *London,* and alongside he added one word: *Loneliness.*

three

William Booth's loneliness would not last forever. The cure for his isolation came in a roundabout way through some changes that were happening in the Methodist church. By 1850, John Wesley, the founder of Methodism, had been dead for almost sixty years. Originally, Methodists had been known for open-air meetings that welcomed everyone—including the poor and destitute. Evangelism and revivals were common. By the time William Booth arrived in London, however, many Methodists were embarrassed by those traditions. Methodist churches were often rigid and stale, and people objected to evangelism—especially among the poor.

Other Methodists held firmly to John Wesley's vision of the church. They were bothered that John Wesley himself might not be welcome in some Methodist churches. So they began what was known as the Reform Movement. They wanted to reform the church from within, but their efforts led to contention within the church. Bitterness and suspicion marked many relationships.

William Booth sought to hold himself aloof from the disputes and divisions, although his friend and former superintendent, the Reverend Samuel Dunn of Nottingham, was one of the leaders of the Reform Movement. William's efforts were doomed to fail. In 1850, the Walworth Chapel, which he attended in London, labeled William a reformer because he had attended some meetings of the Reformers. Because of that label, they took away his class ticket (the equivalent of church membership). William Booth's isolation was complete.

But one man, Edward Harris Rabbits, himself a reformer, heard Booth's preaching and liked it. William Booth was young, fiery, and ardent, pulling no punches. Rabbits encouraged William's preaching and was one of many people to get the young man more involved in the Reform Movement. Rabbits was a prosperous businessman who owned a chain of South London boot stores, and he became a champion for Booth, seeing in the young preacher better things and wider horizons.

One afternoon, Rabbits met William outside his lodgings and coaxed the young man to come with him to a meeting of Reformers.

"A tea party?" William asked.

"Yes," responded Rabbits. Rabbits was anxious to show off William and his oratorical skills at a social gathering. Catherine Mumford had also been invited. She had previously heard Booth preach in Binfield Hall, Clapham, and had related to Mr. Rabbits that she felt it was the best sermon she'd ever heard delivered there. At twenty-three she was so shrewd a judge of sermons that Rabbits was inclined to pay a lot of attention to her judgments.

William Booth, of course, didn't know any of this. But he was impressed with Miss Mumford. When his host asked him to recite an American temperance poem, Booth refused. He wasn't a sociable person. It was the gentle, musical voice of the dark-eyed woman pleading from the sofa that convinced him, albeit reluctantly, to recite "The Grog-Seller's Dream":

> *"A grog-seller sat by his bar-room fire,*
> *His feet as high as his head and higher. . .*
> *Foolish and fuddled, his friends had gone,*
> *To wake in the morn to a drunkard's pain,*
> *With bloodshot eyes and a reeling brain. . ."*

Immediately a noisy argument ensued. One moderate drinker launched into a defense of his habits. Others joined in. Booth must have thought, *Oh my! Now what have I done!* But all Booth remembered was the clear determined voice that rang out above the others, defending the principles the poem set forth. Catherine remembered that when the guests filed into the dining room for supper, the wine remained untasted.[1]

William and Catherine did not talk with each other again until April 1852. It all started when Mr. and Mrs. Rabbits invited Booth to dinner at their home early that month. At the end of the meal, Mr. Rabbits abruptly said, "You must leave business and wholly devote yourself to preaching the gospel."

Booth was incredulous. "There is no way for me. Nobody wants me. Besides, I can't live on air."

"How much *can* you live on?" Rabbits asked.

"Well, let me do some calculating," William responded. After a few moments he said, "Twelve shillings a week would secure lodging and keep me in bread and cheese."

Rabbits pooh-poohed the idea. "Nonsense! You can't do with less than twenty shillings a week, I'm sure. Tell you what I'll do—I'll supply it for the first three months at least."

Anxious to be doing what he felt he was called to do, William quit his job at the pawnbroker's shop and after a lengthy search rented two cramped rooms in a widow's house near the Elephant and Castle Tavern. It was Good Friday, April 10, 1852—William's twenty-third birthday. He next decided to go to a furniture shop and buy a bed, some chairs, and a few other pieces to make himself a usable home in his rented rooms.[2]

That afternoon, Mr. Rabbits bumped into William and invited him to a meeting of Reformers. Catherine Mumford also attended the meeting, and at its close, William offered to escort Miss Mumford home. The lurching carriage ride made small talk very difficult, and he could see that she struggled to speak easily while being jounced around on the carriage seat. He insisted that they not try to converse under the situation—even though keeping up small talk was considered the proper thing to do in such circumstances—and impressed the young woman with his thoughtfulness.

Once the carriage reached Catherine's home in Brixton,

her parents—Sarah and John Mumford—insisted that William spend the night. He already knew that in his few brief meetings with their charming young daughter he had fallen hopelessly in love. The feeling was shared by Catherine, but being a proper young woman, she kept her emotional attachment to herself. The social customs of their day dictated that both William and Catherine avoid talking about such personal issues so early in their relationship.

Catherine's recollection of that evening included these thoughts: "That little journey will never be forgotten by either of us. It is true that nothing particular occurred, except that as William afterwards expressed it, it seemed as if God flashed simultaneously into our hearts that affection which afterwards ripened into what has proved at least to be an exceptional union of heart and purpose and life, and which none of the changing vicissitudes with which our lives have been so crowded has been able to efface. We struck in at once in such wonderful harmony of view and aim and feeling on varied matters that passed rapidly before us. It seemed as though we had intimately known and loved each other for years, and suddenly, after some temporary absence, had been brought together again, and before we reached my home we both suspected, nay, we felt as though we had been made for each other, and that henceforth the current of our lives must flow together." [3]

As William got to know Catherine and her family, he learned that she was born at Ashbourne, Derbyshire, about thirty-five miles from Nottingham, on January 17, 1829. They were the same age. Catherine was one of five children, but only she and her brother John survived infancy. John left for America at age sixteen.

Mrs. Mumford was known as an exceptionally devout woman, and her husband was a wheelwright and carriage builder. Mrs. Mumford, anxious to impress the young evangelist, told him, "Catherine read from the Bible already at age three, and she read it eight times by the time she was twelve."

"Mother. . ." Catherine said, rescuing William from her mother's excessive praise.

When Catherine was four years old, her family moved to the home of Mrs. Mumford's father in Boston, Lincolnshire. Catherine's father became involved in the rising temperance movement, speaking out against drinking alcoholic beverages whenever the opportunity arose. When she was twelve, Catherine became secretary of the juvenile temperance society and wrote articles for temperance magazines.

At about the same time, her mother allowed Catherine to attend a girls' school in Boston. Catherine's mother worried that her children would be corrupted by public schools. She taught them at home. It was only when she became convinced by friends that the girls' school in town was full of teachers who were in agreement with Mrs. Mumford's positions that she allowed Catherine to attend. Catherine enjoyed being exposed to history, geography, composition, and math—subjects that her mother had avoided.

Two years later, Catherine developed a problem in her spine and had to spend the next few months in bed. Her public education was over, but while confined to bed, she studied church history and theology. William Booth was thrilled when he learned that Catherine was well read and that she particularly enjoyed Charles Finney's works on theology and his *Lectures on Revivals of Religion*—William's favorite book.

But Catherine faced other problems besides ill health while she was growing up. She was isolated from other children her age. The only friend she had was her pet dog, a retriever named Waterford. One day, Catherine and Waterford went to see her father at work. Catherine left the dog outside while she went into the shop. She stumbled as she entered the doorway and cried out. Thinking his owner might be harmed, Waterford crashed through the large plateglass window to rescue her. Mr. Mumford was quite angry over what he saw as unnecessary damage to his shop and ordered the dog immediately destroyed.

Catherine was heartbroken. Years later, she wrote of that incident, "The fact that I had no childhood companions doubtless made me miss my speechless one the more."[4]

Her father's extreme reaction to Waterford's accident was typical of his erratic behavior. A man of extremes, he went from being a Methodist lay preacher to simply preaching against drinking. Then he stopped his temperance activities and began to drink heavily. Catherine experienced firsthand the problems that families encounter when alcohol is abused. At the time she met William, Catherine and her mother were still praying that Mr. Mumford would stop drinking and return to his earlier commitments. The pain Catherine suffered as she watched her father deteriorate under the effects of alcohol fueled her opposition to any form of drinking.

One other significant event during Catherine's teen years happened about a year after her family moved to the Brixton section of London. At the age of sixteen, she was in her words "truly and savingly converted." While she had been a good person up to this point, she had no assurance that she was a child of God. "It seemed to me unreasonable to suppose that I could be saved and yet not know it," she later observed.

One morning she happened to glance at the words of a hymn by Charles Wesley: "My God, I am Thine, What a comfort Divine, What a blessing to know that Jesus is mine!" She was quite familiar with this hymn, but the words struck her in a new way. Later she described the experience with these words:

Now [these words] came home to my inmost soul with a force and illumination they had never before possessed. It was as impossible for me to doubt as it had been before for me to exercise faith. Previously not all the promises in the Bible could induce me to believe: now not all the devils in hell could persuade me to doubt. I no longer hoped that I was saved, I was certain of it. The assurances of my salvation seemed to flood and fill my soul. I jumped out of bed, and without waiting to dress, ran into my mother's room and told her what had happened.[5]

Catherine and her mother attended a Wesleyan Methodist church, but they were caught in the divisions between

Wesleyans and Reformers, just as William had been. When Catherine refused to stop attending meetings of the Reformers, she was expelled from the Wesleyan Methodist Church.

"This was one of the first great troubles of my life," she later wrote, "and cost me the keenest anguish. I was young. I had been nursed and cradled in Methodism, and loved it with a love which had gone altogether out of fashion among Protestants for their church. At the same time I was dissatisfied with the formality, worldliness, and defection from what I conceived Methodism ought to be, judging from its early literature and biographies as well as from Wesley's own writings and his brother's hymns. I believed that through the agitation something would arise which would be better, holier, and more thorough. Here were men who, in my simplicity, I supposed wanted to bring back the fervour and aggressiveness of by-gone days. In this hope and in sympathy with the wrongs that I believe the Reformers had suffered, I drifted away from the Wesleyan Church, apparently at the sacrifice of all that was dearest to me, and of nearly every personal friend."[6]

As William and Catherine got to know each other, they discovered they had many common interests as well as common experiences. Their feelings for each other grew stronger. Catherine became a constant source of encouragement to William. In response to a letter from him which must have indicated more than a small degree of discouragement, she wrote:

My Dear Friend,

I have been spreading your letter before the Lord, and earnestly pleading for a manifestation of His will to your mind. And now I would say a few words of comfort and encouragement.

If you wish to avoid giving me pain, don't condemn yourself. I feel sure God does not condemn you, and if you could look into my heart you would see how far I am from such a feeling. Don't pore over the past! Let it all go! Your desire is to do the will of God, and He will guide you. Never mind who frowns if God smiles.

The words, "Gloom, melancholy, and despair," lacerate my heart. Don't give way to such feelings for a moment. God loves you. He will sustain you. The thought that I should increase your perplexity and cause you any suffering is almost intolerable. I am tempted to wish that we had never seen each other! Do try to forget me, as far as the remembrance would injure your usefulness or spoil your peace. If I have no alternative but to oppose the will of God, or trample on the desolations of my own heart, my choice is made! "Thy will be done!" is my constant cry. I care not for myself, but O, if I cause you to err, I shall never be happy again!

It is very trying to be depreciated and slighted when you are acting from the purest motives. But consider the character of those who thus treat you, and don't overestimate their influence. You have some true friends in the circuit, and, what is better than all, you have a Friend above, whose love is as great as His power. He can open your way to another sphere of usefulness, greater than you now conceive of.[7]

William wanted an engagement. Catherine shared this desire, but it appears that she wanted both of them to take a considered look at their relationship before making such a commitment. The reasons she explained in another letter to him, dated May 13, 1852:

My Dear Friend,

I have read and reread your note, and fear you did not fully understand my difficulty. It was not circumstances. I thought I had fully satisfied you on that point. I thought I had assured you that a bright prospect could not allure me nor a dark one affright me, if we are only one in heart. My difficulty, my only reason for wishing to defer the engagement was that you might feel satisfied in your mind that the step is right. I dare not enter into so solemn an engagement until you can assure me that you feel I am in every way suited to make you happy, and that you are satisfied that the step is not opposed to the will of God. If you are convinced on this point, irrespective of circumstances, let circumstances go and let us be one, come what may; and let us on Saturday evening, on our knees before God, give ourselves afresh to Him and to each other. When this is done, what have we to do with the future?

*We and all our concerns are in His hands, under
His all-wise and gracious Providence.*

*Again I commend you to Him. It cannot,
shall not be that you shall make a mistake. Let
us besiege His Throne with all the powers of
prayer, and believe me,*

> *Yours affectionately,*
> *Catherine*

They had known each other eight months. Probably on
Saturday night, May 15, 1852, William asked the Mumfords for their daughter's hand in marriage. The Mumfords
gave their willing consent. Before the new year of 1853,
the two were engaged.

four

The young couple soon faced many decisions. They agreed that they would not try to renew the three-month arrangement with Mr. Rabbits when it reached an end that July, but they were not sure what William should do next.

Both Catherine and William were increasingly concerned with the disorganization and disagreements that marked the Reformers at that time. They discussed at length what they felt was taking place. Although the Reformers had broken with the Wesleyan Methodist Church because of what they perceived to be its deadness and conservatism, the Reformers themselves, with all their committees and the complicated machinery of the movement, were hindering the work of revival.

William recognized that his connection with the Reformers was hampering what he felt to be his real mission. "Catherine, I just don't see this as the place for me. . .for us. . . ."

From July until October, William and Catherine considered becoming Congregationalists. William Booth's reputation had preceded him, so when he sought an appointment with Dr. John Campbell, a well-known Congregational minister, he was warmly received.

"I've heard your life story, young man, and I liked it," Dr. Campbell said. "I like you, and believe the Congregational Church is just the place for you. You will make your way in it, and I will help you all I can."

Dr. Campbell went on to suggest, "Go to college. Study your Bible, and then come out and preach whatever doctrine you honestly believe you find there."

Greatly encouraged, and armed with the names and addresses of other Congregational ministers, William set about to learn what going to college would entail. Not everyone he talked with was as encouraging as Dr. Campbell. One minister recommended that William work for two years under the supervision of another minister before he considered going to college.

Frustrated by what he was hearing, William wrote to Dr. Campbell: "To wait in uncertainty, for one or two years, and then, after that, to be two or three years longer in training ere I could settle down to a sphere of labour, is not in accordance with my feelings or hopes. But even this, should I see it to be the path my Father points out, I am willing to walk therein. All I can do now is to stand still and see the salvation of God."

Dr. Campbell intervened, and William was accepted at the Cotton End Training Institution. But William was still troubled about some theological issues that had been dividing Methodists for decades. Most troubling to William was the Congregationalist belief in election and limited atonement, meaning that God had prechosen those people who were to become Christians and that Christ's death on the cross only atoned for those "elect" people's sins. "I am troubled about the doctrine of election," he explained to the college committee.

The committee advised William to study two books dealing with this issue and other points about which he had some reservations. Nothing William read changed his mind, and he couldn't see himself preaching something that he didn't believe.

"Catherine, I cannot accept Calvinism—that's what it amounts to," he said at one point and with characteristic energy flung the book he had been reading to the other side of the room. "I would sooner starve than preach such doctrines. It would be a waste of time for me to attempt to do so."

William Booth never entered the Congregational College. While wondering what to do next, William received an invitation from the Reformers to take over the Spalding circuit in South Lincolnshire, about a hundred miles north of London. Although he still had reservations about the Reformers, William realized that such an assignment would keep him away from the power struggles and resistance to revivals that appeared to mark so many of the Reformer leaders in London.

Catherine shared William's concerns, and neither one of them was happy about the idea of being separated by such a long distance. But they believed God was leading William to go to Spalding, and in November 1852, William said his good-byes and headed north.

During their separation, Catherine had time on her hands and wrote to William almost daily. He was trudging on foot or rattling in a gig over the flat fenlands of his twenty-seven-mile-wide parish. That left very little time for him to respond to her letters, but Catherine never wavered in her love and encouragement, even though at times she must have felt it was very much a one-way courtship. She was willing to trust the future to God.

During this time, the young couple discovered that they did not see eye to eye on everything. Catherine was an avowed feminist—most unusual for that day. She wrote a strong letter to a minister who had dismissed women as the weaker sex, and she sent a copy of the letter to William as he worked on the circuit. To her shock, William took the minister's part.

Catherine was beside herself. "Oh, prejudice, what will it not do!" she raged. "That. . .woman is in any respect except physical strength and courage inferior to man I cannot see *cause* to believe, and I am sure no one can prove it from the Word of God."

Faced with such a strong reaction from a person whose views he respected, William was forced to rethink his position. In the end, he felt compelled to compromise. "I would not encourage a woman to begin preaching," he wrote bravely, but added, "although I would not stop her on any account. . . . I would not stop you if I had power to do so, although I should not like it."

That letter ended in an agreeable mood: "I am for

the world's salvation; I will quarrel with no means that promises help."

Catherine's letters to William were the lifeline of their long-distance relationship. Travel was difficult, and William couldn't afford either the time or the expense of visits to Catherine. His revival efforts met with much success, not only in Spalding, but in the surrounding district. In spite of the separation, her letters frequently showed the growing depth of her love for him:

My Dearest William,

The evening is beautifully serene and tranquil, according sweetly with the feelings of my soul. . . . All is well. I feel it is right, and I praise God for the satisfying conviction.

Most gladly does my soul respond to your invitation to give myself afresh to Him, and to strive to link myself closer to you, by rising more into the likeness of my Lord. The nearer our assimilation to Jesus, the more perfect and heavenly our union. Our hearts are now indeed one, so one that division would be more bitter than death. But I am satisfied that our union may become, if not more complete, more Divine, and, consequently, capable of yielding a larger amount of pure, unmingled bliss.

The thought of walking through life perfectly united, together enjoying its sunshine and battling with its storms, by softest sympathy sharing every smile and every tear, and with thorough unanimity performing all its momentous duties, is to me exquisite happiness; the highest earthly bliss I desire. And who can estimate the glory to God and the benefit to man accruing from a life spent in such harmonious effort to do His will? Such unions, alas, are so rare, that we seldom see an exemplification of the Divine idea of marriage.

If indeed we are the disciples of Christ, "in the world we shall have tribulation"; but in Him and in each other we may have peace. If God chastises us by affliction, in either mind, body, or circumstances, it will only be a mark of our discipleship; and if borne equally by us both, the blow will not only be softened, but sanctified, and we shall be enabled to rejoice that we are permitted to drain the bitter cup together. Satisfied that in our souls there flows a deep undercurrent of pure affection, we will seek grace to bear with the bubbles which may rise on the surface, or wisdom so to burst them as to increase the depth, and accelerate the onward flow of the pure stream of love, till it reaches the river which proceeds out of the Throne of God and of the Lamb, and mingles in glorious harmony with the love of Heaven.

The more you lead me up to Christ in all things, the more highly shall I esteem you; and if it be possible to love you more than I now do, the more shall I love you. You are always present in my thoughts.

Believe me, dear William, as ever,

Your own loving

Kate

A letter from him in response sounds stilted to our ears, but every word must have been cherished by Catherine:

My own dear Catherine needs not that I should assure her of the affection I bear her. "Actions speak louder than words" is an aphorism often quoted by her, and one that William thinks is fully borne out in his brief acquaintance with her whose eye this may meet. He, the chosen of her heart, wishes her all earth's pure and hallowed joys, promises to increase them as far as he has power, and to aid in the formation and development of that character which is the golden key to unlock the gates to another brighter and happier sphere.

Catherine's letters frequently encouraged William to set aside time for studying. She realized how important it was for any preacher to be exposed to great ideas and great thinkers. She also warned him against letting his popularity in Spalding make him ambitious.

And William was quite popular among the country folk. His ministry flourished, and—most importantly to him—people were being converted. Still, William and Catherine's letters are full of discussions about whether they should stay with the Reformers. They were increasingly convinced that they needed a more stable, less fractious denomination behind them. They were also bothered that revival services were being seriously hampered by the unsympathetic attitude of many churches.

One group that particularly appealed to both William and Catherine was the New Connexion. Started in the

1790s, shortly after John Wesley died, the New Connexion had a strong Wesleyan theological base, supported revivalism, and included laypeople in decision making. William and Catherine believed all three of these characteristics were important. Like many people of their day, their views on how churches should be run were being influenced by the movement toward democracy in society at large.

At first, William wanted his circuit of churches near Spalding to join the New Connexion. When the quarterly meeting of the circuit voted against joining, William determined to join as an individual. He still faced many options. The members of the Spalding circuit wanted him to continue and offered him a home, a horse, and the ability to get married immediately as enticements for staying with them. They knew that the New Connexion had a standard probationary period of four years before a new pastor could get married. Some friends recommended that William simply step out as an independent revivalist without any ties to a particular denomination. Reformers in London asked him to take over the Hinde Street circuit with an annual salary of one hundred pounds.

Eventually, William decided to join the New Connexion. In February 1854, he resigned from the Spalding circuit and applied to the Reverend William Cooke for candidacy in the New Connexion ministry. He had heard of Cooke's seminary at Camberwell, South London. Cooke was thorough—indoctrinating students against what the Wesleyan Methodists termed "worldliness"—and he drilled his students through lessons in elocution, grammar, rhetoric, logic, composition, church history, and elementary Latin and Greek.

William worked hard at his lessons, but he did not enjoy them. He couldn't see how studies in Latin would help him be a better minister. However, William relished opportunities to do practical mission work in the neighborhood. Cooke would attend and later critique his students' sermons.

The first time Professor Cooke listened to William preach, the professor's daughter attended as well. At the end of the sermon when William invited those who wanted a relationship with Jesus to come forward, Professor Cooke's daughter was one of the people who responded.

Years later, William recounted Professor Cooke's response: "The next morning was the time for examination and criticism of the previous day's work. . . . 'Well, Doctor,' I said, 'what have you to say to me? You heard me last night. What is your judgment on my poor performance?'

" 'My dear Sir,' he answered, 'I have only one thing to say to you, and that is, go on in the way you have begun, and God will bless you.' "[1]

Another benefit to attending Professor Cooke's seminary was that William was once again in London and could see Catherine much more often. Later that year, William was accepted into the New Connexion and told that the four-year probation before marriage usually given to new pastors would be shortened to only one year in his case.

Neither William nor Catherine were idle during that year. Catherine wrote the first of what were to be hundreds of magazine articles. Published in the *New Connexion Magazine,* the article presented ideas on "the best means for retaining new converts." She also continued her voracious reading habits and correspondence with William and other friends.

William was at first appointed assistant superintendent of the London circuit and then made a traveling evangelist. His college training may have been limited, but what he lacked in certain areas of preaching, he made up for in his passion for souls. That was why he entered the pulpit. As he traveled the countryside, William often spoke to thousands of people at one meeting.

When his one-year probation ended in May 1855 and he returned to London to get married, it had been more than three years since William had asked Catherine to marry him. Later she cautioned young people against rushing into either engagement or marriage. As a young girl she had made up her mind on four qualities which she regarded as indispensable to the character of the man she hoped to marry.

"In the first place, I was determined that his religious views must coincide with mine. He must be a sincere Christian, not a nominal one, or a mere church member, but truly converted to God."

The second qualification concerned basic common sense. The third spoke to the biblical, theological, and cultural mandate that was most critical in her way of thinking, "a oneness of views and tastes." Finally, Catherine had resolved never to marry a man "who was not a total abstainer, and this from conviction, and not merely to gratify me."[2]

William met all four of Catherine's standards, and at the end of their three-year engagement, they were more than ready to begin a life of ministry together.

five

The wedding took place on June 16, 1855, at the Congregational Stockwell New Chapel, South London. It was a small, quiet affair, followed by a one-week honeymoon at Ryde on the Isle of Wight, just off the southern coast of England.

Rest and relaxation did not last for long, however. William had new responsibilities to take up. Earlier that spring, Josiah Bates, an important New Connexion layperson in London, had suggested that William be appointed as an evangelist for the entire denomination throughout England. During the annual conference of the New Connexion, held one month before William and Catherine's wedding, William was appointed as a full-time, traveling evangelist.

Immediately following their brief honeymoon, the couple sailed across the English Channel to Guernsey, one of the famous Channel Islands located close to France.

Catherine dreaded sailing and was ill much of the time during their stay in Guernsey, but she was determined to be with her new husband as he began his revival meetings.

No sooner had they completed a successful series of meetings throughout Guernsey but they sailed across to Jersey, another Channel Island. There they held another series of revival meetings before sailing to southern England and making their way back to London. Because of friends and family in the capital city, London would remain the young couple's home base.

Catherine continued to be ill, and it was clear she could not always travel with her husband as he spoke throughout the country. Her parents were more than willing to have their only daughter stay with them, so when six weeks after their wedding William set out for a speaking engagement in York (about 175 miles north of London), Catherine stayed behind. The separation so soon after their wedding was hard on both William and Catherine, and they both wrote many letters to each other. William's letters were filled with descriptions of the work he was doing, and Catherine's contained generous amounts of advice.

Having recovered her strength, Catherine joined William for his next three series of meetings, held in cities a little south of York. They ended up in Dewsbury, where they stayed for a month. By that time, the rigors of travel had again brought illness. Catherine's lungs were inflamed, and she couldn't attend William's services. According to her letters to her parents, she treated her illness with homeopathic medicine, "by which I have been spared the misery of blisters, purgatives, and nauseous doses, and the tedious weeks of convalescence attendant on them."[1]

Homeopathic treatments had become popular in Victorian England and in many cases were certainly an improvement over the standard treatments of the day. Catherine's adult life was marked by a fascination with homeopathy, vegetarianism, and other alternative treatments advocated for improving health. By the end of the Booths' four-week stay in Dewsbury, Catherine was feeling much better and was able to attend the last meeting in the Wesleyan Chapel. More than two thousand people crowded together to hear William speak.

Catherine's letters to her parents during this period present her marriage as stable and happy. She only voiced two concerns. One, of course, was both hers and William's health. Life on the road was hard on both of them. The other concern was the understandable wish for a place to call home. It was difficult to continually unpack their belongings in the housing provided for them, live there for at most a few weeks, and then pack everything up and move on. But Catherine was convinced that she and William were doing God's will. In a letter to her parents in October 1855, she wrote, "With the exception of the drawback of a delicate body and being without an abiding home, I have all I want."[2]

Flush with exhilaration from the success of the meetings at Dewsbury, William and Catherine traveled about ten miles northeast to Leeds. Here they settled in for the Christmas season and stayed through January 1856. During all these travels the newlyweds stayed in other people's homes where there were usually small children underfoot. It gave Catherine ample opportunity to observe, as she wrote her mother, about how children should and should not be trained. She formed definite opinions which were to be put into practice with their own offspring. Her interest in the subject was probably intensified by the fact that she was expecting a child. Although pregnancy was not openly discussed in polite society during those days, Catherine and William were excited about the prospect of adding to their family.

During the two months spent in Leeds, more than 800 conversions were recorded. When the meetings concluded, Catherine insisted on a brief vacation. Another letter to her parents shows her concern for William's well-being: "It will be thirteen weeks on Saturday since we left Chatsworth, and he has had no rest since, so I have taken the matter into my own hands, and for no power on earth will I consent to any more toil until he has rested a bit. We leave here all well next Friday, and go to Huntslet to spend a week at one of the principal friends."

In commenting about this, biographer Roger Green points out that there may have been some disagreement over this matter, for William dropped a note to Catherine's parents informing them that "she gave me a curtain lecture on my 'blockheadism, stupidity,' etc. . . . However, she is a *precious,* increasingly precious treasure to me, despite the occasional dressing-down that I come in for."[4]

After that it was on to Halifax, another town near Leeds. They always remembered their two months in Halifax because it was there, on March 8, 1856, that their first son, William Bramwell, was born. He was named after a well-known English evangelist, and from birth, the child was expected to fit in with his parents' mission. "I had from the first infinite yearnings over Bramwell," Catherine stated in later years. "I held him up to God as soon as I had strength to do so, and I remember specially desiring that he should be an advocate of holiness."[5]

Shortly after Bramwell's birth, his parents took him along to their next meeting place. Word had been sent to Catherine's parents about the birth of little Bramwell, and Mrs. Mumford traveled up from London to assist in the care of the baby. It was during this time that William was reappointed as an evangelist for the New Connexion.

Marriage enabled Catherine to better understand the consuming zeal that prompted William to "the necessity of labouring for the salvation of souls," as he described it in one of his early journals. She also saw that he was a man of many doubts, and that his joy and enthusiasm over results masked some deep anxieties. He was, after all, human. She became his champion. Writing to her mother, she said, "If God spares him, and he is faithful to his trust, his usefulness will be untold, and beyond our capacity to estimate."

The young family traveled throughout the Midlands of England. In the industrial city of Birmingham, William began to use street meetings for evangelistic purposes. The next two years were packed with travel and meetings, including a series of revivals at Nottingham, William's birthplace. At times, Catherine and the baby would stay with her parents in London while William continued his revivals.

While William was well received wherever he went, he also found some critics. Chief among those was P. J. Wright, who agreed to let William speak throughout his circuit, but then criticized his methods. Some of his objections were probably a reaction to the emotionalism that often appeared in revival services. He may also have been suspicious of the techniques William used in organizing and conducting the meetings.

William and Catherine were both impressed by the methods of evangelism laid out by Charles Finney in his book *Lectures on Revivals of Religion,* published in 1835. Finney believed that a properly structured service would virtually guarantee a positive response to the gospel. It is clear that William adopted some of his practices directly from Finney and combined others with patterns of teaching and evangelism that had existed in the Methodist movement from the time of John Wesley, nearly a century before.

But Wesley's methods were no longer appreciated by a number of leaders in the New Connexion. In the spring of 1857, the Annual Conference of the Methodist New Connexion was held at Nottingham. P. J. Wright and others who were uncomfortable with William's methods removed him from his position as a full-time evangelist for the denomination. By a vote of 44 to 40, he was directed to take a regular circuit and focus his energies on a full range of pastoral responsibilities. This, it was argued, would give William important experience in administrating a circuit before he was ordained. However, those who pressed this new assignment on him certainly understood that it would leave the Booths little time for evangelism.

To make matters worse, William and Catherine were assigned to the New Connexion circuit at Halifax, more than 160 miles northwest of London and far removed from the places where they were known and liked. Among those familiar with the denomination, the circuit was considered both obscure and unsuccessful—the perfect place to bury two troublemakers.

Frederick Booth-Tucker, a son-in-law of William and Catherine, referred to the superintendent of the Halifax circuit as "a sombre, funereal kind of being, very well-meaning no doubt, but incapable of cooperating with Mr. Booth in his ardent views and plans for the salvation of the people."[6]

Catherine, whose health deteriorated after the move, said of Brighouse, a smaller town just southwest of Halifax where they were assigned living quarters, "It is a low, smoky town, and we are situated in the worst part of it."[7]

Surprisingly, despite ill health and personal misgivings, Catherine's work with the girls and women at Halifax prospered. Roger Green, one of her most thoughtful biographers, considers this to be the true beginning of her public ministry.

The best that can be said for William was that he endured the year at Halifax.

At the annual conference of the New Connexion in the spring of 1858, William was finally ordained. He and Catherine were encouraged to discover that several important circuits were competing for their appointment by the conference leadership.

William was assigned to Gateshead, a town of fifty

thousand located just across the river Tyne from New-castle, on the northeastern coast of England.

From the beginning, the Booths saw the town of Gates-head and all its surrounding communities as part of their ministry. They immediately organized a series of revival meetings and began experimenting with new ways to publicize them. They distributed handbills from door to door throughout entire neighborhoods. Street meetings were organized, featuring hymn singing that alternated with short invitations to attend the services later in the day. An entire day was set aside for prayer before the meetings began and other times of prayer were woven into the services themselves.

During the next year, the membership of Bethesda Chapel, the main church in the Gateshead circuit, in-creased from 39 to 300. Though its 1,250 seat capacity made it quite large for its day, the chapel often lacked enough room to hold all the people who were eager to experience William's dramatic presentation of the gospel. During the services, all eyes were on him as he paced back and forth across the platform at the front of the church. His strong and enthusiastic voice reached to the farthest corners of the building.

Catherine was deeply involved in all aspects of the work from the beginning. She prayed publicly in the first Sunday service, something that was almost as con-troversial for a woman to do as preaching. She also taught class meetings that included both Bible study and carefully structured times for personal examination and accountability.

Almost by accident, she began to visit homes in the

poorer parts of town and was soon devoting two evenings a week to this work. She was deeply moved by the suffering and want that she discovered there.

"The plight of the women is so pathetic," she often remarked to her husband.

It was not long before Catherine's work among the poor was generating nearly as much comment as William's preaching.

The people of Gateshead soon began calling Bethesda Chapel "the converting shop," because they were so impressed by the work that both of the Booths were doing in their midst.

In spite of the success of that first year, William found himself chafing under the restrictions placed on him by fixed circuit responsibilities. Much of Gateshead was a bleak, lower-class suburb, attached to a larger industrial area. Many who lived there did not feel comfortable in churches full of wealthier and better-educated people. William gradually became concerned about reaching those who never darkened the door of the chapel. John Wesley's eleventh rule for his helpers began to haunt him: "You have nothing to do but save souls. . . . Go always not only to those who need you, but to those who need you most."

As he looked out over the monotonous rows of dark slate roofs, William would often say to his wife, "Kate, in how many of those houses is the name of Christ never mentioned? Why am I here, with this crowded chapel of people who want to hear the message? Why am I not outside, bringing the message of God to those who don't want it?"

Catherine had helped William fight off discouragement

before, so she was not surprised by his frustration.

She chose her words carefully. "William, you *are* out there. You're out in the circuit probably far more than you should be. How can you possibly do any more? You have all the parish work here, and then you stretch yourself and go to these other places. I am concerned for you, my dear. How much can one man do? Give God time, William, give yourself time. It won't always be this way."

During the annual conference of the New Connexion, in the spring of 1859, William was reassigned to Gateshead and given permission to expand his evangelistic work.

Catherine's public ministry also continued to grow, and she soon had an opportunity to strongly and publicly defend the right of women to preach the gospel.

In the fall of 1859, Phoebe Palmer, already widely known in England and America through her books *The Way of Holiness* and *Faith and Its Effects,* conducted a series of meetings in the Newcastle area. She was immediately attacked by the Reverend Arthur Augustus Rees, an independent minister in the town of Sunderland, near Gateshead. He spoke out against her from the pulpit of his church and also published a pamphlet ridiculing women preachers in general and Mrs. Palmer in particular.

This deeply angered Catherine Booth, and before the end of 1859 she had produced a pamphlet entitled *Female Teaching: or the Rev. A. A. Rees versus Mrs. Palmer, Being a Reply to a Pamphlet by the Above Named Gentleman on the Sunderland Revival.* In it she vigorously defended both the right and the duty of women to preach.

The pamphlet was reprinted in the fall of 1861, with

revisions that strengthened her arguments. Her unwavering commitment to the idea that women should be involved in all aspects of God's work was to have far-reaching consequences for the roles of women in The Salvation Army.

During these years, William and Catherine added to their family. The first four of their eight children were born between 1856 and 1860. They also continued to learn more about each other. William discovered that while Catherine was a parlor intellectual and could hold her own with anyone, her desire and willingness not only to talk, but to participate, was real. She was able to discuss current trends in the churches of England, she was aware and greatly concerned about the revival and anti-revival movement that had been taking place, and she understood the plight of the poor throughout much of England.

Were it not for her, he acknowledged time after time, he could never have fulfilled his great life's work. When his heart ruled him, she was cool, levelheaded. She provided fresh reasons for battling on when black despair or self-pity seized him. She was his equal in zeal, capacity for hard work, and sacrifice. She was both a stimulant and a stabilizer to her gifted husband.

What was it like for Catherine Booth as the mother of so many little children? Did she experience the usual frustrations and fatigue that goes with motherhood? Her son Bramwell provided answers to these questions: "In my boyhood I have sometimes known her exceedingly harassed by the cares of a house full of children, and tried, no doubt, by straitened circumstances, and by her own bodily weakness. I have seen [Father] come into the house, put his hat down in the hall, and, entering the room, find it all out in a moment. Taking her hand, he would say, 'Kate, let me pray with you,' and he would turn us out while they knelt together. Then a little while after it was evident that the skies were blue again."[8]

Catherine was convinced teaching obedience was key to child rearing. "Obedience to properly constituted authority is the foundation of all moral excellence, not only in childhood, but all the way through life. And the secret of a great deal of the lawlessness of these times, both towards God and man, is that, when children, these people were never taught to submit to the authority of their parents; and now you may convince them ever so clearly that it is their duty, and would be their happiness to submit to God, but their unrestrained, unsubdued wills have never been accustomed to submit to anybody, and it is like beginning to break in a wild horse in old age. . . . The great majority of children are ruined for the formation of character before they are five years old by the foolish indulgence of mothers."[9]

Catherine's writings are a reflection of her speeches; they are compelling and heart-touching, practical and loving. As famous as her husband was, Catherine herself was soon to become known throughout England as "the woman preacher."

six

Although Catherine Booth's fame as a woman preacher was destined to endure for twenty-eight years and to spread far beyond Gateshead, many leading Methodists shook their heads. It was just too inappropriate. Unbiblical, too, they determined.

Shortly after writing her pamphlet that defended Phoebe Palmer, Catherine wrote *Female Ministry: Woman's Right to Preach the Gospel*, which was published in 1860. She argued persuasively that women's "graceful form and attitude, winning manners, persuasive speech, and above all, a finely-toned emotional nature" ideally equip them for public speaking. And, if the consequences of the Fall included set occupations, men should "till the ground" as God commanded. But, Catherine argued, if men escape drudgery to find refined tasks, why should women be confined to "the kitchen and the distaff" on account of Eve's sin? She denied the charge that "female ministry is forbidden in the Word of God."

"Whether the Church will allow women to speak in her assemblies," she wrote, "can only be a question of time; common sense, and public opinion, and the blessed results of female agency will force her [the church] to give us an honest and impartial rendering of the solitary text on which she [again, referring to the church] grounds her prohibitions. Then, when the true light shines and God's Word takes the place of man's traditions, the Doctor of Divinity who shall teach that Paul commands woman to be silent, when God's Spirit urges her to speak, will be regarded much the same as we should regard an astronomer who should teach that the sun is the earth's satellite."

It was this urging to speak which she felt to be from the Holy Spirit that saw Catherine Booth get up on Whitsunday, May 27, 1860, as her husband was concluding his sermon, and walk slowly down the aisle to where he stood. Perplexed, but all solicitude, he was at her side, meeting her.

"What is it, my dear?" He was fearful that she was ill.

A buzz of whispered comment arose from a thousand voices. Mrs. Booth was kindness and gentleness personified and, in fact, she was considered rather timid, if not downright bashful. But all that was to change. They were about to come to know another side of the Reverend William Booth's wife!

"William, I desire to speak."

Possibly no one was more astonished than her husband. She had argued with herself before leaving her seat, *You will look like a fool and have nothing to say*. She quickly recognized this as the devil taunting her. *You have overreached yourself,* she thought, but then retorted inwardly: *That's just the point. I've never yet been willing to be a fool for Christ. Now I* will *be one!*

Still in a state of shock, Booth announced meekly, "My dear wife wishes to speak." Then he sat down.

"I dare say many of you have been looking on me as a very devoted woman, but I have been disobeying God," Catherine began. She didn't hesitate, the conviction in her heart rising to her lips as she spoke out: "I am convinced that women have the right and duty to speak up, yes, even to preach. I have struggled with this for a long time, but I'll struggle with it no longer. . . ."

Many in the congregation, especially the women and young girls, began to weep. It was their moment, too. William had a swift and practical mind, and as he observed what was happening, he acted on his thoughts.

He quickly hastened to his wife's side as she finished speaking. They consulted only briefly. Then, striding to the pulpit, he announced, "Tonight my wife will be the preacher!"

That was the beginning. From then on, Catherine occupied the pulpit in many places. If she was considered "a fool" or if any other unkind words were directed against her in the years to follow, it didn't matter. She had declared from the outset that she was willing to be a fool for Christ, if that's what it took, and she never wavered or backed down in her commitment to speak the truth and obey what she believed to be God's leading.

Catherine's preaching was one more controversial element in the Booths' ministry that many leaders within the New Connexion found offensive. A year later during the 1861 annual convention, the memorable scene took place where Catherine proclaimed from the gallery, "No, never!"

At first, William and Catherine acquiesced to the convention's decision for William to serve in the Newcastle circuit. He was an assistant to help with the pastoral work, and William hoped this would leave some time for evangelism. Accepting the new assignment also solved the problem of where the family would live if they immediately withdrew from the New Connexion. With the difficulties of the yearly conference behind him, William hoped to find some way to get the support he needed for the work he felt so strongly called to do.

Still, he felt trapped. As he said to Catherine shortly after his appointment was confirmed, "I feel cribbed, cabined, and confined by a body of cold, hard usages, and still colder and harder people."

In June 1861, the Booth family moved to Newcastle. William soon found that he had to look outside the denomination for preaching opportunities because many New Connexion pastors were afraid to incur the wrath of his enemies by showing any support for either William's or Catherine's work.

As always, Catherine tried to bolster her husband's crumbling morale: "We must not give up. God loves us. He will sustain us."

Though Catherine had lost all patience with the New Connexion, she also understood William's hesitation to leave, when they had no place to call home and no way to make a regular living.

In a letter to her mother she wrote: "I am so nervous, I can scarcely write. We don't know what to do. And yet God knows we only seek to do the right. . . . I am willing to trust God, and to suffer, if need be, in order to do His will."

In another letter she seemed to be trying to reassure herself that risk-taking was a necessary part of a living faith. "I have no hope that God will ever assure us that we shall lose nothing in seeking to do His will. I don't think this is God's plan. I think He sets before us our duty, and then demands its performance, expecting us to leave the consequences with Him. If He had promised beforehand to give Abraham his Isaac back again, where would have been that illustrious display of faith and love which has served to encourage and cheer God's people in all ages? If we could always see our way, we should not have to walk by faith, but by sight. I know God's professing people are generally as anxious to see their way as worldlings are, but they thus dishonour God and greatly injure themselves. I don't believe in any religion apart from doing the will of God. True faith is the uniting link between Christ and the soul, but if we don't do the will of our Father it will soon be broken."[1]

Apparently she was looking for some definitive indication of God's will, both for herself and for William. As she wrote later in the same letter, "If my dear husband can find a sphere where he can preach the Gospel to the masses, I shall want no further evidence as to the will of God concerning him. If he cannot find a sphere I shall conclude that we are mistaken. But I cannot believe that we ought to wait till God guarantees us as much salary as we have hitherto received. I think we ought to do His will, and trust Him to send us the supply of our need.

Anyhow, I am convinced the Lord will guide us, and I am willing to stand by my dear husband, and do all I can to help him in whatever course he may decide upon."[2]

On July 16, 1861, William received a letter from Dr. Crofts, passing on to him a reprimand from the Annual Committee of the New Connexion. This group governed the denomination between annual conferences, and it included a large number of men who disapproved of the Booths. The letter claimed that William had not yet begun acting as a pastor for the Newcastle circuit.

Soon after the letter arrived, Catherine sat her visibly shaken husband down. Hand on his arm, she leaned forward earnestly and said, "To postpone action any further will be an act of disobedience to what we both sense is 'the Divine will' of God. William, don't hold back because of me. I can trust in God and go out with Him, and I can live on bread and water; go out and do your duty. God will provide, if we will only go straight on in the path of duty."

It was finally clear to William that there was no way to make peace with the New Connexion. Two days later, he sent his letter of resignation to the Reverend H. O. Crofts, D.D., president of the Methodist New Connexion. In part, William's letter stated:

> *You ask me to tell you "frankly" what I intend to do. I reply that all the way through my conduct has been open and frank in the extreme. But once again I say that I intend to be an evangelist, if it be possible; and if, after a fair trial, I fail in reaching that sphere, I will give it up, and conclude that I have been mistaken, but not till then. . . .*

Therefore, intensely painful though it be, . . .I place my resignation in your hands. . . .

I do this after much prayerful deliberation. I know what I am sacrificing, and I know I am exposing myself and those whom I love to loss and difficulty. But I am impelled to it by a sense of duty to souls, to the Church, and to God. Were I to quail, and give up for fear of the difficulties which just now appear to block my path, I feel sure that I should in the future reproach myself with cowardice in the case of my Master, and that even those who differ with me in opinion would say that I was not true to the professions I made in the Conference, when I said I had offered myself to the Lord for this work if I went forth "without a friend and without a farthing."

Trusting in God alone, I offer myself for the evangelistic work, in the first instance to our own Connexional churches, and, when they decline to engage me, to other portions of the religious community. I offer myself to cooperate in conducting special services, or preaching to the outlying crowds of our population, in theatres, halls, or the open air.

Looking at the past, God is my witness how earnestly. . .I have endeavoured to serve the Connexion, and knowing that the future will most convincingly and emphatically either vindicate or condemn my present action, I am content to await its verdict.[3]

One further difficulty faced them. Since William's resignation had to be accepted by the annual conference, it wouldn't take effect for ten months. Their position became, in Catherine's words, "About as trying as it well could be."

Once the news of William's resignation got out, their friends were quick to offer support. At one tea meeting they were affectionately applauded.

Shortly after this incident, Catherine reported, "I feel happier this morning than I have for three months past. I feel as though my dear husband stood forth as an honourable and unflinching Christian before the world, and I am proud to help him to face the difficulties which frown upon our path. I verily believe God will clear our way and smile upon our work. He knows our motives."[4]

Now that the break was final, William felt free to set down his misgivings about the entire New Connexion movement without hesitation or apology: "I was satisfied that the methods of the average Methodist Church were out of date. They had ceased to attract the people to the Church—at any rate, in the city. . . . I was not satisfied with the chapel itself, with its dull grey walls, detached life, class pews, and high-toned preaching, far beyond the thoughts of the people. I was dissatisfied with my own work. I saw grow under my ministry warm, loving, soul-seeking Christians; and then I saw them chilled, neglected, and killed. I rebelled against the repetition of this work."

Within a few weeks, the family moved to London to live with Catherine's parents. While the grandparents took care of the children, the two Booths set out to establish an independent evangelistic work.

In spite of her desire to leave the New Connexion, Catherine also understood the risks of this venture: "So, now the step is taken, [and] we both intend to brace ourselves for all its consequences and manfully face all difficulties. The Lord help us and show us His salvation!"[5]

Their first invitations to preach came from a young minister who was one of William's early converts. The Reverend Mr. Shone had worked with the Booths at Gateshead and lived with their family for a year. He was now the pastor of a New Connexion congregation at Hayle, in Cornwall, a county in the farthest southwest corner of England. He pointedly requested that both William and Catherine come and hold services, thus putting himself at some risk within the denomination. Not only was he inviting William, but he was also asking Catherine to preach.

The revival work there began on Sunday, August 11, 1861. The original plan for seven weeks of meetings quickly expanded to a mammoth eighteen-month campaign, unparalleled in that part of England since Wesley's day. The work included many meetings in other parts of Cornwall and involved both New Connexion and non-New Connexion Wesleyan groups.

Catherine described this time as "the most remarkable awakening" ever to occur in western Cornwall. At least seven thousand Cornishmen found peace with God. Catherine found herself accepting invitations to preach and conduct revival meetings as often as William did, though she preferred to accompany him whenever possible.

It was reported that fishermen rowed ten miles across dark and choppy seas to hear the Booths preach. It was not unusual for villagers to walk for miles to attend the meetings. Businessmen reported a sharp decline in commerce of all kinds as shop owners and customers alike participated in the revival. Everywhere they turned, William and Catherine found an undeniable hunger for God.

From Hayle, the Booths went to St. Ives and conducted meetings from the end of September 1861 to the middle of January 1862. Their children rejoined them, and it was a time of great success, with 1,028 people converted or renewing their commitment to Christ. Among that number was Catherine's father. After years of praying for her father to return to Christ, Catherine was filled with joy.

But not all the news was good. They also learned that the Wesleyan Conference had forbidden them the use of its chapels.

Later, in St. Just, thousands were brought to the Lord and Catherine could write, "The windows of Heaven were opened, and a shower of blessed influence descended upon us." Catherine began holding meetings for women only, where she shared her views on such issues as fashion, child rearing, and adoption. She also used these times to comment on the important social problems of the day and to stress the importance of women's involvement in the church at all levels. Her audiences often included many who were wealthy and socially prominent. Catherine believed that they had a special responsibility to relieve the suffering of the poor.[6]

She felt no hesitation in making very blunt statements to them. One of her best-known sayings was, "It will be a happy day for England when Christian ladies transfer their sympathies from poodles and terriers to destitute and starving children."[7]

71

The Cornish revivals continued in various other places until the late fall of 1862. During that time, two significant events took place. First, during its annual convention, the New Connexion officially accepted William's resignation and passed a resolution banning the Booths from Wesleyan pulpits. Second, their fifth child, Herbert, was born on August 26.

Early the next year, William and Catherine began a series of meetings at Cardiff, in Wales. They were denied access to the main chapels in the area and so were forced to find new places to hold the services. They rented a large, indoor arena and also used a circus tent. This was considered a radical departure at the time, but it created unique opportunities for them to reach people who did not feel comfortable in church buildings. When derelicts and prostitutes were converted, William's joy seemed particularly profound.

The Booths soon concluded that people who lived in a world of saloons and honky-tonks often found a tent flap more inviting than the heavy door of a stately church. They also discovered that these secular surroundings had advantages for the Christians who came to the services. Without the visible signs of denominational loyalty to remind them of their differences, many believers began to experience a sense of unity in Christ that had been almost unknown to them before.

Friendships were established at Cardiff that would be critical to the development of the Booths as individuals and to the success of their ministry for years to come. Wealthy shipowners John and Richard Cory were deeply moved by what they saw and heard at the services. They quickly offered to underwrite the expenses of the work. Later they would provide critical financial support during the early days of The Salvation Army, support that would continue for fifty years. Marian Billups would become a lifelong friend to Catherine, and both she and her husband would be important early supporters of The Salvation Army.

William and Catherine were not the only ones worried about the resistance that kept appearing to revivalism in England. Charles Spurgeon, the well-known Baptist preacher, commented on it in an article published by the *Baptist Almanac* in 1863.

In "A Call to the People of God," he wrote: "The present state of our Churches fills me with alarm. The gracious revivals of the last few years were indications of the Lord's readiness to work in the midst of our land. . . I fear that we have slighted a golden opportunity which may not return while any of this generation are alive. . . . Communities which despised the revival are confirmed in their sin by its manifest subsidence. . . ."[8]

In spite of all their success, this was a difficult time for William and Catherine. Bramwell, their eldest son, has written the following about his father during these years, but it could just as easily be applied to Catherine:

> *For two years after the Churches were thus closed against him, he wandered about the country without a religious domicile. . . . Those two years were probably the darkest in his whole life, at least from the time of his ordination onwards. Small buildings only were available for his*

73

> *services—he who had been accustomed to great*
> *congregations. . . . Yet this period, dark and per-*
> *plexing as it was, was a period in which, I con-*
> *sider, he was being most marvellously fitted for*
> *the work which, unknown to him, was awaiting*
> *his hand in the East End of London.*[9]

The road that led the Booths to the East End of London began with necessity. They were thirty-two years old and had five children. Living expenses needed to be met; children had to be fed and clothed; a roof had to be kept over their heads. No longer did they have the parsonage for their home, the baptismal and marriage fees, and other advantages of the settled clergy. They would need two incomes. She would do what needed to be done. Itinerant evangelism was a hard way to make a living, but make it they would. The nature of this work may have been unstable, but God was their stability.

They chose Leeds, a town in the English Midlands, as their first permanent residence in three years. Here their sixth child, Marian Billups Booth, was born on May 4, 1864. This daughter's birth brought sorrow into the home because she became an invalid and suffered some degree of mental retardation. The exact reasons are not clear: A younger sister said that Marian had smallpox at an early age which left her an invalid, unable to study; her brother-in-law Booth-Tucker said that Marian had convulsive fits shortly after birth and remained an invalid; and a biographer of William Booth said that Marian was an invalid because of an accident which left her with serious physical weakness. All agreed that she was unable to take part in public life, and all three explanations may have contributed to this fact. With the help of governesses, however, Catherine kept right on with her preaching.

It was at this juncture that William and Catherine decided they could increase their effectiveness for the Lord by conducting separate campaigns, so Catherine began conducting revival meetings on her own. Catherine wrote of this difficult time, "Our course out of the churches and downward to the masses must be continued."

To help ease some of their financial insecurities, the Booths sold a hymnbook they had published, along with Catherine's pamphlet *Female Ministry* and books and pamphlets from revivalists and others with whom they were in agreement. But the uncertainty of their income created financial stress, even though they trusted God to supply their needs.

Catherine accepted invitations to preach in South and West London, wealthy areas of the city. Wherever she went, she experienced the joy and satisfaction of seeing results. Converts filled the aisles. Catherine was formidable in the pulpit and with the press. Hundreds of adults and children made professions of faith under her ministry at that time.

In February 1865, Catherine, who was a Londoner by inclination, eagerly accepted the invitation to lead revival services in the smoky dockland parishes of Rotherhithe and Bermondsey, in southeast London. William had been holding revivals in the north of England.

The exceptional success of Catherine's meetings, which ran through the middle of March, created the opportunity for more speaking in London. In order to accommodate her many London engagements and allow her to be at home with their children during the evenings after preaching, William and Catherine leased a house in London. This also brought the family nearer to her parents.

It was Catherine's preaching along with the success William was having ministering to poor people which came to the notice of the *Revival,* England's premier revival journal. In early 1865, editors Richard Cope Morgan and Samuel Chase wrote to William that they were interested in having him preach in Whitechapel, a poor section in the notorious East End of London, in spite of the fact that William allowed his wife to preach.

"We agree to female preaching in principle, but doubt that a mother should forsake her home duties," they wrote. The couple had become accustomed to hearing this concern expressed.

In spite of their differences on the subject of women preaching, William accepted the invitation to preach to the East End in July. This introduction to the appalling depths of irreligion and physical misery of the poor in London was to grip him like nothing else had done before.

Throughout 1865, opportunities for Catherine's preaching were coming from many places. The Midnight Movement for Fallen Women, an agency that combined evangelism and social redemption, contacted her. She responded, and it was this organization which opened her eyes to the need for evangelism to be allied with social concern. "The sickness and destitution are indescribable," she informed her husband. "Seven-year-old girls work fourteen-hour days, with only the whiplash of an overseer's strap to keep them awake. The brothels. . .oh, the poor women. . . And the children, victims of cholera and smallpox. I was told about the plight of the matchbox makers of Bethnal Green where in one house children from four to sixteen years of age were at work, one, a boy, with a broken spine, was putting sandpaper on the matchboxes, and he could only work kneeling.

"In another house there is a dying mother watching three children at work. And I heard about a child of not quite four who worked five hours a day; another who worked from 10 A.M. till 9 P.M. . . ."[10]

The Midnight Movement for Fallen Women was to go on to help support the ministries of the Booths for years. It was a providential association.

In ongoing efforts to help support their family and feeling at all times that she was responding in obedience to the call of God, Catherine increasingly held meetings. By the end of the year, some of those meetings were in London's largest halls, lasting as long as three months. Her West End work to the materially wealthy but spiritually poor was growing.

A woman far ahead of her times, Catherine saw the need to champion the cause of women and elevate them to places of responsibility and usefulness in Christian endeavor. Through her preaching in the West End, Catherine was touching the hearts and lives of people who could provide support for the struggling work in the East End. She minced no words. Never once did she hold back. She turned the tables on comfortable, affluent Christians, insisting that they were responsible for the sweatshops, for employing women and children in filthy working conditions at the lowest wages possible.

According to Roger Green, "Indeed, much of the blame for the poverty and thievery of the East Enders she laid at the feet of her audiences in the West End."[11] William Booth was fully supportive of her work and touchingly devoted to her. She may have earned the label "the woman preacher," but she was his adoring wife and the mother of his precious children. There was mutual support throughout their growing ministry. Catherine and William remained friends as well as lovers throughout their thirty-five years of married life, and there is every indication that their love and respect for each other increased with the passing of the years.

seven

"Kate, I really have but one aim," he stated that Sunday evening in July 1865 when he arrived home, dead tired, but needing to talk. She had put the children to bed and sat up waiting patiently for her husband to turn the key in the lock.

Kissing and hugging her, accepting the tall glass of water from her, he said, "I know you share this with me, but let me clarify—I want for us to continue to be instrumental in converting the outcasts the clergy and the churches aren't reaching. Then, I would like to pass them on to the churches so they can nurture them in their new-found faith. But, my dear, as you and I know, that hasn't happened and I doubt very much that it will happen. There has to be some other way. We must find it."

They were now thirty-six. Upstairs their six children—Bramwell, aged nine, to Marian, just fourteen months—slept peacefully, as yet untroubled by the problem of winning bread from a hard world.[1]

An awful realization had dawned upon William Booth. An invitation from the East London Special Services Committee to preach at a small revivalist mission and at their Quaker Burial Ground tent that first week of July in nearby Whitechapel had led him to postpone a campaign in Derbyshire. This was an opportunity to be nearer home —with Catherine and the children—for a week.

The meetings, however, had been well attended and the Special Services Committee asked him to stay on. Their encouragement, plus the numbers of drunkards, thieves, gamblers, prostitutes, and pleasure seekers who were turning out to hear him, provided an irresistible pull.

Thousands flocked to Mile End Waste, a mile-long strip of broken ground between the pavement and the main Mile End Road, that sultry summer. Walking in their midst the tall, dark-bearded stranger, his Bible beneath his arm, attracted curiosity at first. He was an imposing figure, likened, in fact, to the way one would have expected an Old Testament prophet to look, and he commanded attention by virtue of his long stride.

Now he stopped outside a drab, red-brick tavern. He read the sign: The Blind Beggar. He drew out a book from his dark frock-coat pocket and read the verse of a hymn. The tone of his voice was high, and instantly faces appeared at the pub's windows.

A ragged unwashed throng began pressing about this six-foot, one-inch stranger wearing a wide-brimmed hat. He seemed like a towering giant. His face was pale, he had a long straight nose and a firm chin, and his grey eyes were piercing in their intensity.

The Bible now was open in his large hands. "There is a Heaven in East London for *everyone—for everyone who will stop and think and look to Christ as a personal Savior.*"

An ever-widening circle of people was now pressing around him, and he could tell that some were listening. They sensed something different about this man—his voice had a ring to it; it was the sound of love which they, as yet, couldn't identify. But it did hold their attention.

"Someone threw a rotten egg at me, Kate," he said, apologizing for the smell and the stain on his frock coat, as he handed it to her. "I told them where they could come for the services at Whitechapel and at the Quaker Burial Ground tent, but I doubted that I would see many, if any of them there. As I left them and walked through the Mile End Road, my dear, I saw terrible sights—ragged, shrieking people, little children foraging for food, dirty women, some clad only in soiled petticoats, more little children—these appeared drunk with their mothers forcing beer down their throats—whimpering, hungry dogs, men's faces with animal passion written all over them as they watched dancing women in the street.

"I've been told that there are 3 million souls in London, and 100,000 paupers. After what I've seen this week, I know it is true. And they did come to the meetings.

"Many of those people are on the brink of starvation. As I came further west, towards here and you and the children, a conviction grew within me. In the alleys, Catherine, the people are sick, some of them are dying, some are already dead. And the smell. . .the whole city stinks. I couldn't escape it. . . ." He shuddered in remembering.

81

"I know, William, oh, my dear, I know," she said, placing her arms around his shoulders, comforting him.

"But Kate. . . Oh, my sweet love of a wife, how can I ask this of you? Where can you go, if you were to travel the world, and find such heathen as these—and where is there so great a need for our labors? I have been asking myself all the way here tonight, 'Why go to Derby, or anywhere else, to find souls who need the gospel?' "

The cold of uncertainty clutched at her heart even as she heard her husband say, "Darling, I've found my destiny. It's a human jungle out there," and he waved his long arms. "I've been walking in the midst of it. . . . It's as bad as any tiger-infested jungle in darkest Africa."

As he'd walked, the conviction had mounted within him—these were people going to a Christless eternity. He and Catherine could and must do something for them.

"The salvation of the soul is the key to salvation of the body," William Booth insisted, and he preached it fervently on every occasion when he met with those who had the wherewithal to help bring about change. They would need all the help they could get. They were no strangers to hard work and self-denial.

To herself Catherine was thinking: *This will mean another move, another start someplace else. . . . How can we possibly hope to make a living among poverty-stricken East Enders? Who will go to bond for us?* Her questions were not that of a doubter, although she had every reason, humanly speaking, to doubt. She was expecting another child—it would be their seventh—and they were already making do on so little.

"Yes, I think you need to stay on in East London,

William," she heard herself say. "If you feel you ought to stay, stay."

That was the beginning of a grueling life for William. He was appalled time after time by the misery of the East End slums. He would trudge eight miles from Hammersmith to the East End every day for evening meetings and each Sunday for services, and then once his work was done, he'd walk the eight miles back home. Ever more frugal, William's lunch consisted of bread and cheese eaten from a paper bag in James Flawn's refreshment rooms in Pudding Lane. Flawn was an early convert, and he would make the bone-tired Booth a cup of cocoa. Having filled his stomach, William would stretch out on a back room sofa until it was time for another service.

The winning of East Enders to Christ was a bitter uphill struggle. He told Catherine upon returning from a meeting, "Oh, Kate, as I passed by the doors of the flaming gin palaces tonight I seemed to hear again a voice sounding in my ears, 'Where can you go and find such heathen as these?' Kate, I can't get away from the conviction that I must stay and preach to these East End multitudes."

Sometimes his clothes were torn; one night he came home with bloody bandages swathed around his head. "A stone or something hit me pretty good," he said apologetically as she gently removed them and cleaned the wound. Another night someone had taken offense at his preaching and hurled him against a curbstone. The rowdyism of the East London mobs was almost unendurable, but Booth was a man on a mission.

For six weeks he held tent meetings nightly and three

times on Sunday. These were preceded by open-air services on Mile End Waste opposite the Blind Beggar pub in Bethnal Green. Then, leading the way, he would march to the tent with the people marching in procession after him. He was, as it were, once again the pawnbroker's boy leading the roughs to Broad Street Chapel.

William loved these people; they felt it, they saw it, and they responded. As many as fifteen penitents came forward each night, certainly not the kind of numbers to which he had become accustomed as he traveled the revival trail, but a significant inroad nonetheless.

The evangelical press began to take notice and started publicizing his work. The *Revival* carried a letter from W. Jones Hayden, an influential member of the Special Services Committee, to John Stabb, another man of influence on the committee, commending "the labors of our dear Brother Booth."

"They are responding to the love of God that they see in you, my dear," said his darling Kate.

"William, we have always trusted the Lord for our support; we can trust Him again." She reiterated what by now had become a familiar refrain.

But he was concerned for his family's welfare. After speaking for ten weeks in Peckham in early 1866, Catherine again fell ill, and it was necessary to take her to Tunbridge Wells in Kent to recuperate. It was a hard blow to their finances, but it also proved providential in more ways than one. While there, they met Henry Reed, a wealthy retired Tasmanian sheep farmer and Wesleyan churchman who invited William to preach at his mission in Dunorlan, his palatial estate. Prior commitments to the East End made it necessary for William to decline, but Catherine was able to accept. Her preaching so impressed Reed that he opened up his checkbook and became a loyal supporter until his death in 1880.

Returning to Whitechapel, William plunged into the work among his beloved outcasts with increased fervor.

eight

S ometime in September 1865, William Booth received what he could only see as confirmation of the new work to which he felt he and Catherine were called. A few weeks earlier, he had sent an account of what was taking place in the East End to Samuel Morley, a Liberal member of Parliament for Nottingham—someone whom apparently Booth knew about from his Nottingham days. He hoped his letter would inspire Morley to provide some much-needed financial aid.

Morley summoned William to his office and handed him a check for one hundred pounds. "This is for your family expenses, William," he said. "I am hopeful that other friends will rally to your support and recognize that what you are doing is so important."

Booth had also asked others for help, and that aid was forthcoming. Enthusiastic and feeling certain this was a sign of God's blessing and leading, he went to Catherine.

"I am confident we can do it," he said. "We will move forward. And we will move," he added. "Kate, I need to get closer to the work."

Thus it was that in November 1865, William was able to relocate his wife, their six children, and their Irish maidservant, Mary Kirkton, to No. 1 Cambridge Lodge Villas, Hackney, East London. The move was made none too soon, for on Christmas Day, their seventh child, Eveline Cory (named for their Welsh friends and benefactors), was born. In later life, she would be known as "Evangeline."

Eveline's arrival was special. That Christmas Day brought weather in London that Dickens might have described. Snow lay on the ground, and it drifted around the trees and bushes, a beautiful sight, a wintry wonderland. The six children of William and Catherine Booth were playing together in the parlor of their new home. The door opened and their father came in. He carried a hamper, and with great expectation the children jumped up and ran to him. "Here is the Christmas gift we've been waiting for," he announced.

Carefully he pulled the covers back slightly, just enough so they could see the new baby's face. "It's a little sister for you," he said. A new baby on Christmas day! Squeals of joy and excitement mingled with questions.

"What's her name, Father?" one of them asked.

"We shall call her Eveline Cory Booth."

She was to go down in history as the first woman general of The Salvation Army, succeeding her father and her brother, but that was still a long way off.

The family moved only once more, three years later, to

No. 3 Gore Road, Hackney, where they lived for twenty years. This was a larger home, in a quieter, more peaceful neighborhood that was better suited to Catherine's physical ailments. The home served as a kind of second headquarters for William's growing work. Their busy lives never allowed for the privacy Catherine so cherished, but despite the incredible growth of the new work they launched in 1865, and the enormous demands on his time, William Booth loved to spend time with his wife and children. They were a happily united family, but home life was always at a premium. The children's favorite game was "Fox and Geese" with their father always playing the fox.

Another favorite game had no name, except in Booth children parlance, and they called it "getting Papa on his feet." His lank frame—six feet, one inch—presented a challenge for the children. He, of course, gave them a little help as he raised himself somewhat from the floor, and then would relapse into a dead weight, slumping heavily back amid the squeals of joy from all the little ones.

There was the children's card game, "Snap," with Papa joining in, shouting just as loudly as any of the children, his long white fingers dealing the cards.

The children had their share of pets—guinea pigs, white mice, birds, dogs. Eveline even had a marmoset (a monkey) that she tried dressing to look like her father. When her mother gently said, "But, Eva, it doesn't live the life," she gave up on the rascal.

William Booth had a fun-loving nature that showed itself with his family. He would even assemble rabbit hutches and join in their excitement as the children welcomed new little bunnies. He sang loudly as he dressed in the morning and would run swiftly up and down the stairs, much to his children's entertainment.

It was, by today's standards, an old-fashioned Victorian home—no drinking, no tobacco, no dancing, no evenings at the theatre, no days at the racecourse. There was little make-believe—everyone was too busy with their real beliefs. But life was not all repressive negatives; the home was filled with the exhilaration of their father's work as the ardent leader of what was first called "The Christian Mission." Their home was always open to zealous evangelists and visitors.

The Booths were never affluent, and their poverty caused Bramwell, their eldest son, to object. When his mother patched his clothes, he said, "The boys will laugh at me. They'll think we are poor."

"Well, so we are," his mother responded with her typical honesty. But she talked it over with him, and in later years, he was able to put her philosophy in these words: "She not only patched our clothes, but made us proud of the patches."

The children loved reenacting the age-old dramas of the Bible—David and Goliath, Noah and the ark, or Daniel in the lion's den. Their craving for realism and their father's flair for the dramatic may have influenced their efforts at preparing the burnt offering mentioned in the Book of Leviticus. One biographer stated that no French polisher in London could have restored the charred surface of the nursery table!

Ballington, the second son, fancied himself as a preacher when he was eleven years old. He enlisted the help of Kate, aged ten, and Emma, aged eight, to come with their dolls to his services. When the "babies" fussed, Ballington ordered sternly, "Take those babies out of the theater." His sisters, triumphant, pointed out, "Papa would not have stopped—Papa would have gone on preaching."

In despair, Ballington would turn his attention to a convert—usually a pillow propped up in a chair. "This is a good case," he would enthuse, lugging the convert/pillow toward a makeshift communion rail. "Give up the drink, brother."

Bramwell recalled his father taking him as a teenager into an East End pub. Gas jets played eerily on men's inflamed faces, drunken, disheveled women were openly nursing their babies, and the reek of gin and shag tobacco, along with the smell of sweating bodies, almost nauseated the young man. Seeing the look on his son's face, William Booth said quietly, "These are our people. These are the people I want you to live for and bring to Christ."

nine

Having made the decision to focus William's ministry in east London, the Booths created The East London Christian Revival Society, later to be known as The East London Christian Mission, and subsequently as The Christian Mission. "Caution and careful organization must be exercised," Catherine counseled at the outset.

Realizing that William would not be paid for any of his work initially, the family relied on gifts from friends and money earned by Catherine when she spoke to the wealthier West Enders. At this point, Catherine's work was better known in London society than were her husband's efforts among the poor in the East End. In fact, Catherine was the primary promoter and publicizer of The East London Christian Revival Society.

A statement in the *Christian Mission Magazine* (January 1877), under the heading "Origin of The Mission," described William's decision to work in the East End:

Mr. Booth was then [1865] a perfect stranger in the neighborhood and had no intention of remaining in London; but so evidently was the seal of the Divine approval impressed on these services and so immensely important did it seem to him that something should be done to reach with the Gospel the teeming thousands who seemed to be outside the pale of all ordinary religious agencies that, after much deliberation and prayer, he gave himself up to this department of labor.

The *Wesleyan Times* (August 20, 1865) gave this brief but positive testimony reporting on the success of the early meetings at the tent:

The Reverend William Booth has been engaged for the past seven weeks holding a series of special meetings in the East End of London near the London Hospital and in the Mile End Road. Hundreds of working men and numbers of persons who never enter any place of worship have listened night after night to appeals of this devoted servant of God, and many conversions have taken place. The work is assuming a permanent character and a large hall in the neighborhood is about to be engaged for the winter. . . . In no part of the Metropolis is there greater need for an evangelistic effort.

What is considered the registration of the birth of The Salvation Army was made at this time by Booth in a letter sent to the *Revival* on August 17, 1865. Of course the organization was not yet named The Salvation Army, but in terms of continuity of purpose, this could be considered its birth. The letter set out the deplorable spiritual condition of the population of East London, and continued:

As announced by one or two correspondents to your valuable paper, I have been engaged in an effort in this direction (the employment of extraordinary means to make known to the people of East London the love of God) the last six weeks. Invited by Messrs. Stabb and Chase I held a week's services in a large tent erected in the Quakers' Burial Ground, Thomas (Vallance) Street, Whitechapel; and so evident was the Divine approval that the services have been continued until now. Nearly every night two meetings are held, first in the Mile End Road, and afterwards in the tent; and on the last two Sabbaths we have conducted four services each day. We have held two very successful tea meetings, charging 3d. each for admission. There have been but two or three meetings of the whole course at which sinners have not professed to find mercy, and sometimes thirteen or fourteen have done so in the one evening. . . . We have no very definite plans.

We shall be guided by the Holy Spirit. At present we desire to be able to hold consecutive services for the purpose of bringing souls to Christ in different localities of the East of London every night all the year round.

We propose holding these meetings in halls, theaters, chapels, tents, the open air, and elsewhere as the way may be opened or we seem likely to attain the end we have in view. We purpose to watch over and visit personally those brought to Christ, either guiding them to communion with adjacent and sympathetic churches or ourselves nursing them and training them to active labor.

In order to carry on this work we propose to establish a Christian Revival Association in which we think a hundred persons will enroll themselves at once. We shall also require some building in which to hold our more private meetings, and in which to preach the gospel when not engaged in special work elsewhere.

For the most part, simple people of limited ability responded to Booth's call for help. The giants of forceful leadership would come later. In those early days, William Booth stood quite alone at the head of the army that was in the making. He had hoped for an enlistment of a hundred who would stand with him; the actual number was only sixty. And after the first year, many of those left for one reason or another—some found his teaching on the truth of sanctification not in keeping with their own beliefs; still others considered that he laid too much stress upon repentance and good works. His way of conducting prayer meetings gave offence to some, and others didn't like the penitent form. But it was mainly the mocking and mobbing by the crowds in the streets that was too much for the endurance of the less zealous. And, in all fairness, it should be acknowledged that some left because they had intended to serve a limited time until sufficient converts had been made to take their places. They then returned to the other Christian organizations which had loaned them for this groundwork.

Booth's insistence upon a definite decision for Christ and out-and-out consecration to His service was so strong that no one could be comfortable under his leadership who was not prepared to go all the way with him in applying these principles to the work which he felt so strongly they were called. The sifting out of the objectors and faint-hearted was necessary. What remained were earnest and consecrated workers who stood by William Booth through thick and thin. Those who became a part of the work later did so with full knowledge of its standards and methods; and in fact, this is what attracted them.[1]

How did the early desertions of workers affect William? The records show that he just went to work more vigorously, seemingly undismayed. He wasn't dependent on numbers; his source of help and strength was the Holy Spirit.

He had already figured out that if he was going to attract the wayward, it wouldn't come through "churchy" music. His people were repelled by the lovely sounds coming from church organs. What they understood and enjoyed came from the twanging banjo, the mellow guitar, the blaring trumpet, and the big bass drum.

"Okay, Kate, if that's the kind of music they like, we'll give it to them," he declared. So he set out to recruit followers who were musicians. If they weren't able to play an instrument, he provided cymbals so they could participate.

With a few musicians and loyal followers, Booth marched to open-air meetings or to the revivals in the Quaker Burial Ground tent. Never mind that along the way they might be bombarded with stones, tomatoes, eggs, dead rats and cats, or other missiles by drunkards and hecklers. He held his Bible high, inviting people to follow, and proclaimed the gospel of love.

He found, however, that he was encountering a persistent problem. One night while addressing an audience of twelve hundred or so at Whitechapel, many of whom were openly vicious, he saw that he was making only a trifling impression. He turned to an old gypsy hawker, converted a few weeks earlier, and said, "Come on up here, my friend, and tell these people what's happened to you."

The old man came alongside William Booth and slowly began his simple faltering testimony. An unnatural quiet fell upon the meeting. The old man was able to explain the promises of Christ in a manner that was compelling, and the rough crowd listened to every word. The aisles were crowded with repentants and first-time converts.

That night William said to his son Bramwell (calling him by his nickname), "Willie, I shall have to burn all those old sermons of mine, and go in for the gypsy's." Courageously, William acknowledged the lesson learned, and from that point on every meeting found converts sharing their testimonies.

To his wife he confided, "The Savior didn't command His apostles to be preachers of sermons; He sent them forth as witnesses of their experience of saving grace. I must do no less."

Catherine shared in this discovery. "Yes, He made Matthew, the publican, an apostle. Look at what He did for Peter! This will be revolutionary, William, but you have seen the results. Yes, do it!"

For her part, Catherine continued to preach to wealthy audiences. Someone suggested that she travel to the seaside resorts during the summer because so many affluent Londoners escaped the heat of the city by moving to the resorts. Catherine thought this sounded like a sound idea, and she and William agreed that during the summer of 1867 she would take the children to Margate. The children were ecstatic to be able to spend the summer by the ocean, and Catherine gained many contacts—some of whom became supporters of William's work.

William's converts, men and women alike, had little in common with the well-connected people Catherine spoke to. His East Enders were typically former drunks, thieves, prostitutes, and other notorious characters. They unashamedly spoke of their newfound liberation in Christ—their freedom from that which had so enslaved them. Drunks-turned-sober gradually made an impression upon other wayward souls who, one by one, would leave the jeering opponents to join the ranks of the penitents alongside the Reverend William Booth.

There was Mother Moore who was won from alcoholism by Booth's passionate oratory. She had been a drunken Whitechapel charwoman. Everyone on the streets knew her. She became famous for her classic retort to someone who offered her a pint of ale: "I can drink of the wells of salvation—and so can you!"

There was Thomas Haywood of Bethnal Green, a twenty-five-year-old alcoholic. John Allen, converted in a meeting at Millwall Docks, single-handedly converted two hundred seamen at Cardiff where Booth had appointed him to go and work.

Many, if not most, of the converts were nearly illiterate. Early testimonies were certainly unique. But they all shared one theme—Christ's love had found a way to reach them, and now, armed with that same love, they pleaded with audiences to come to Christ.

"I am no scholar, my dear friends," one man led off in a crowded meeting. "You must just take it rough, as it comes from my heart."

Another pleaded, "If you only knew how happy the Lord makes us, you would at once come to Jesus."

It was religion for the masses. Handbills began to be passed out, advertising who would be speaking: "The Converted Pigeon-Flier," "A Milkman Who Has Not Watered His Milk Since He was Saved."

The nightly forays into the streets continued, often with a likelihood of someone being subjected to some kind of physical abuse. It was dangerous work. But these were not men and women who would ever again be content to tread the middle road through life. Conversion found them renouncing the world and taking up the cross to follow Christ.

"Come drunk or sober," one handbill advertised. And in Bradford, Yorkshire, astonished neighbors watched a newly converted man return to his home with Johnny Lawley, a mill-hand turned evangelist, roll a barrel of beer out of his house, and tip its contents down the gutter.

It was at the penitent form (what was called the communion rail or mourner's bench in the churches), that men and women knelt, risking ridicule to confess their sins. They resolved to live their lives for Christ. William knew that this system forced individuals to acknowledge their problems wholeheartedly and to accept what Christ offered in exchange. Here the transformation of souls took place. One man, after serving his sentence for murdering his wife, knelt at the penitent form but didn't know what to say. At last, with tears streaming down his face, his mind retraced the lonely years to an almost-forgotten childhood, and he was heard to whisper, "Lord Jesus, forgive me. I have been naughty. . . ."

Kneeling alongside these men and women, in the throes of their conviction, were the men of William Booth's army, those who themselves had come from darkness to light, from misery and hatred to love. They understood.

William knew how important it was to keep track of converts. They must be checked on to prevent them from stumbling. His earlier techniques—most of which had their origin in his youthful Nottingham days as a lay preacher included once-weekly visits, prayer, and encouragement, showing these new converts from the Word of God what was necessary for walking with the Lord.

He needed helpers. Observing the differences between the volunteers who seemed unable to connect with the new converts and those volunteers who were more successful, William recognized that the working-class people to whom he ministered were most influenced by their friends and neighbors—people who shared their experiences. This conclusion was to have great effect upon his future work.

ten

A mong the first converts made at the tent as a result of William's work was an Irish pugilist, a professional boxer named Peter Monk. He met William Booth on Whitechapel Road, and was so impressed by William's appearance and the few words he spoke to him that Peter Monk made up his mind to go and hear William preach.

Monk was booked for a prizefight that night, which he won, but the next day, even though everyone was making him out to be their hero, he wouldn't listen to them. He was determined to go out to Mile End Waste to hear "that preacher." Monk later described what happened: "There he was holding forth surrounded by the blackguards of Whitechapel, who in them days were the greatest vagabonds you could meet anywhere on God's earth. Some were mocking, some were laughing; but Mr. Booth, he shouted at them finely, and then gave out a hymn, and led the singing till he just drowned their noises, or nearly so. Then I threw off my coat and walked round the ring instead of joining in the revelry, and in two minutes all those blackguards were as quiet as lambs.

"And not very long after that he had me down at the penitent form after one of his sermons in the tent."

Peter Monk became William Booth's self-appointed bodyguard. Certainly God was watching out for William, who often walked through dangerous neighborhoods at night. Monk eventually became known as "the general's boxer."

Another outstanding example of loyalty to the work God had commissioned for the Booths came through James Flawn, the man who owned the refreshment room where William stayed and rested between meetings. He was already a mission worker when William Booth first took charge of the tent back in 1865. In giving an account of what he had done to reach street gamblers and drinkers, Flawn revealed something of his own past: "I once was a gambler myself. The dominoes and dice and ninepins were my gods, and the public house parlor and skittle ground were my favorite haunts."

Flawn served on various committees that had to be set up to manage the affairs of the mission. Later, when soup kitchens and relief work became so much a part of Salvation Army work, Flawn directed those efforts. He told an interviewer in 1897 that "the fortnight's campaign at the Tent [in July 1865] was so marvellous in its results that it was by special request extended indefinitely, and crowds—godless, heedless crowds—packed the Tent till one stormy night it was blown to ribbons."[1]

Courageous efforts were made by Booth and his helpers to continue to use the tent, even though more than once its roof was brought down by forceful winds. During one storm, the roof collapsed while about forty people were kneeling, seeking salvation. Another time some of the ropes gave way, but the meeting continued with William directing from the platform, "Go along, my brothers, pull the tent up while I carry on with the preaching!"

Peter Monk insisted that some roughs had cut the ropes. Whatever the cause, the tent was finally beyond repair. It had to be removed and damage to the ground upon which it had stood had to be repaired. The records of the early mission work state that Booth paid in full for the tent's removal.

In the early years of William Booth's work in the East End, he determined that drunkenness was a close ally of poverty and vice. London's numerous pubs laid end to end would have stretched a full thirty miles. In East London alone, the heart of Booth's territory, every fifth shop was a gin shop. Most of these shops kept special steps to help tiny children reach the counter. A feature of the pubs was penny glasses of gin for children. Child alcoholics roamed the streets. Children less than five years old knew the raging agonies of delirium tremens and often died from cirrhosis of the liver. Children could be seen trudging through the streets, bringing gin to parents who lay drunk in their squalid surroundings. These were the by-products of a one-hundred-million-pound-a-year trade. Victims of alcoholism lived only for the next drink.[2]

Seventy years before Alcoholics Anonymous came

into being, William saw alcoholism for the sickness that it was. Satan would have to be battled within his own strongholds, and any means was justifiable, William decided, if it would attract sinners to listen to the message of salvation. Many special techniques were inaugurated to enable Booth and his helpers to reach the hopeless, the debased, and the neglected elements of the community. Thus it was that as the work grew, the music and street parades attracted increasing crowds of people who scorned the regular churches.

"Why should the devil have all the best tunes?" William replied when chided for appropriating the music of popular tunes for his hymns. William Booth was an intensely practical person, and early on he recognized the importance not only of what came to be called "Hallelujah Bands," but the need for what he called "good singing." To please him, singing had to be congregational, hearty, and useful. In speaking at the 1874 Conference of the Christian Mission, William explained his position: "The devil only allows us the crumbs that fall from his table, such as the old hundred[th], and a few more funeral ditties. Of the soul and citadel of music he has taken possession. . .and with it he charms and chains and sways the world.

"But if sensual worldly satanic music wields such a power, what might music not do when songs and hearts and voices were inspired and directed by the Holy Ghost. . . . That is a problem that has yet to be solved. . . . Let us swell louder and louder our triumphant songs, and to the sound of that victorious music let us go up to the conquest of the world for Jesus."

The saying that "the devil has no right to all the good

tunes" has been attributed to both William Booth and Charles Spurgeon. But it was George Scott Railton, who was to become William's lieutenant general in 1873 and was well-known as an author and songwriter, who concluded an article "About Singing" (1874) with this impassioned plea: "Oh, let us rescue this precious instrument from the clutches of the devil, and make it, as it may be made, a bright and lively power for good!"

From the outset, the Mission took advantage of special seasons and festivals—Christmas, New Year, Easter, and bank holidays—for holding meetings. By 1877, the practice of singing in the streets on Christmas Eve had become so much a part of their work, that William felt it necessary to issue special instructions for those taking part in it. It was stated, therefore, that such singing must be exclusively for the glory of God and the salvation of souls and not for the gratification of any man or men.

Seeing how prevailing drinking habits formed such a wretched background to every other kind of misery and were indeed the cause of a great deal of it, William and his people determined to follow Christ's command to "Go out quickly into the streets and lanes of the city, and bring them in." They sought out those who so desperately needed help, whether these people were to be found on the streets, in saloons, or in the hovels that were supposed to be their homes.

The opposition encountered was incredible. A mighty battle was being waged. Their foe was crafty, subtle, and vicious. As the converts increased, so did the antagonism of the pub owners, who were losing some of their best customers.

"That old fool wants to take away the only pleasure you 'ave," the saloon keepers warned their customers. "You can't be like them rich toffs wot spends their money for the ballet and flipperies and such. We're poor people, we are, and we've got to stick together like poor people should."

The argument was forceful. It was quite literally true— the pubs were the social recreation centers for the low-paid working class. What other options did they have in those days? There were no movies, no television, no home videos, no other forms of entertainment as inexpensive or satisfying as a flagon of ale or a few gulps of whiskey.

Booth's mission was to do what he could to help these men and women see that providing a better living for their families and trusting in Christ to help them would provide the happiness they craved. The bulging pockets of the liquor barons were depriving them of a wonderful way of life.

One writer of that era wrote: "Everybody is drunk. Those who are not singing are sprawling. The sovereign people are in a beastly state."

It was a fitting commentary. The beer shops could be open legally from four in the morning until ten at night. Since the Beer Bill of 1830, making beer easy to obtain, the people of Great Britain had experienced thirty years of untempered beer drinking. This had produced the generation of drunkards with which William Booth and the Christian Mission were surrounded.

An article in the *Nonconformist* (November 4, 1868) described what was happening with William's work in East London:

105

*In the Whitechapel Road within a distance of
half a mile, nearly 19,000 persons may be seen
to enter the public houses on the Sabbath Day
while on Saturday evenings the number is even
larger. This place is surrounded by the most
hideous vice, the most dreadful crime, and the
most abject misery. The scenes of drunkenness
and debauchery to be witnessed here almost
exceed belief. The crowded gin shops and public
house concert rooms go far to explain why
poverty and misery reign supreme.*[3]

Men who knew the craving for liquor from infancy were
transformed by the grace of God through the faithful work
of William and his early followers. One such fellow was
Jimmie Glover, an illiterate potboy, reduced through drinking to sleeping in pigsties. When Catherine Booth learned
of Jimmie, she requested that whenever she traveled by
train he accompany her. The coach became a classroom,
and on these trips he learned to spell, read, and tell the
time. For thirty years he was a loyal worker and follower
of the Booths.

Rodney "Gipsy" Smith was, when Booth found him,
more accustomed to washing in dew and sleeping in wheat
fields, but as a seventeen-year-old convert, he became
acquainted for the first time with beds and washbasins. He
went on to become a world-renowned evangelist greatly
used of God.

Uninhibited converts, sensing their burdens of guilt and
lust being lifted from their shoulders, would shout, "I *do*
believe—He *does* save me!" Halfway through the service,

when one man who was overpowered with joy cried, "I must jump," an evangelist urged him, "Then jump."

One night three men and a woman, standing outside a saloon and shouting the glories of the Lord, were suddenly rushed by men carrying boxes of garbage which they dumped over the heads of the four workers.

"Father, forgive them," one man said.

"God bless you and make you see the light," the woman told the attackers.

"Hallelujah!" another man shouted.

The garbage heavers laughed and yelled. The quartet began to sing one of their songs, and the attackers closed in, shoving the four down the street.

This was an all-too-typical episode among Booth's followers, although some of the encounters were even more violent. Hired goons broke up street services by beating the converts. Parading workers were stoned, some were trampled, some smeared with whitewash; many had their faces bloodied. They continued marching to their meeting halls and held services while jeers, insults, and objects were thrown at them.

eleven

C atherine was busy mothering the children and doing her share of speaking to groups who were providing funds to help keep William's ministry going. Her campaigns took her throughout London and as far afield as the eastern and southern coasts of England. The strain of travel and the campaigns themselves took a great deal of energy.

Wisely, the Booths decided that it was in the best interests of the children's health, as well as that of Catherine's, that they not be exposed to all that took place in the East End. The two youngest children had been born in 1865 and 1868, and Catherine herself was in delicate health. But William and Catherine wanted to share everything with each other, so he gave her regular reports about what was happening with the Mission.

A common theme was William's conviction that they needed a building for indoor meetings. The longer he worked with the people in the East End, the more he appreciated how reluctant they were to attend traditional churches. And remembering some of the reactions he'd seen back when he had brought poor converts to church when he first moved to London while in his early twenties, William could sympathize. No one wanted to go where they were not welcome. Besides the need for a location where new converts could be discipled, William also was concerned about the ever-present distractions during outdoor meetings.

"But every outdoor service, Kate," he insisted, "should, if possible, be connected with an indoor meeting. There are too many dissipating influences which more or less always accompany the outdoor preaching, especially in the East End streets. We need indoor meeting places where we can set forth the claims of the gospel with more clarity. We need to hold prayer meetings, and we need to be able to hold personal conversations with the people. Yes, we need space where we can have uninterrupted use."

They found such a place initially in an old wool store in Bethnal Green. It was packed with people for the first meeting, but as was to happen frequently, the meetings could last for only two weeks. Out of that meeting place, however, came a convert, Joseph Fells, who was to be a lifelong supporter of the work of William Booth.

At the time of the forty-third anniversary (1908) of the founding of The Salvation Army, Fells described the procedure of those early days:

The central figure in the Mission was, of

course, the General. Tall and dark, with one corner of his Inverness cape flung back over his shoulder, he presented a striking picture. I never knew him to fail in gathering and holding an East End crowd.

One night on Mile End Waste an infidel lecturer made several attempts to break up the meeting. Finally, he agreed to wait his turn until the close. The crowd, however, followed the little procession to the hall, and the infidel, at first very much exasperated, followed too. The result was that he got converted.[1]

After the wool store was no longer available, the Mission obtained the use of a dancing academy. Joseph Fells remembered that location very well for it was here that his son, Joseph, aged twelve, and daughter, Honor, fifteen, became converts. Mr. Fells remembered that

For the first two months we used to march along the footpath from the Waste to the Dancing Academy, passing on our way a number of public houses whose custom it was to serve drinks outside to men sitting at little tables.

As the procession swept by, these places were invariably deserted by the customers, which naturally annoyed the publicans [the owners of these places]. They complained to the police, and on the Sunday following an inspector tapped the General on the shoulder and told him that the procession would not be allowed to traverse the pavement anymore. So we marched in the road through the Mile End Toll Gate. And the crowds still followed.

Although the Dancing Academy was often uncomfortably crowded, all sorts of plans were used to attract fresh people. One of these was the carrying in the procession of half-a-dozen boards on which were printed in bold letters such warnings as "Prepare to meet thy God."

Honor Fells became Mrs. Booth's maid in 1867. Then in 1869 she married another convert of the Mission named Burrell. Burrell died in 1876, and two years later Honor became an evangelist at the Christian Mission. Later she married again, becoming Mrs. Salthouse. She continued assisting in local work at Manchester until, at more than ninety years of age, she died in December 1938.

Joseph Fells Jr. eventually had charge of one of the five "Food for the Million" shops which was begun by The Salvation Army. He was an active prayer leader, exhorter, and worker until his death at the age of seventy-five.

The stories of this brother and sister are typical examples of the loyalty engendered by the Booths and their work. Thousands of similar stories could be told of individuals and couples who, from the outset, became an active part of the work, continuing as long as they were physically able.

The location and tenancy of buildings used by the Mission throughout the last half of the 1860s and into the 1870s is a long story, and some of the information is unclear.

As resourceful as he was, William Booth and his followers continued to be driven from one rallying point to another, seeking to establish themselves. It was a dogged advance across a no-man's-land of lost souls.[2]

Renting suitable buildings was a big concern. A dancing room, available only on Sundays, seated 350. Friends helped move benches into the hall early on Sunday mornings. In the afternoon William preached on Commercial Road, followed by another meeting indoors. From 5:30 to 7:30 P.M., missioners, as many of his workers were called, conducted a service on Mile End Road, followed by a procession down Whitechapel Road to the hall, all the while singing. At the crowded hall's evening service, William and other workers went from seat to seat, inviting people to accept salvation.[3]

The Mission used whatever facilities it could find, whenever they were available. The Pavilion and Oriental Theatres, a stable in Hosiery Place, a hayloft in a court leading to Redman's Row, the East London Theater, the Pigeon Shop, the Effingham Theater, another old wool store, and the Union Temperance Hall (among many other buildings) appear in documentation portraying the early history of the Mission movement. These people were fighting for a footing in a difficult area.

At one point the Mission was using eleven different halls, mostly on weeknights, and the dancing room on Sundays. These became mission stations, a way for the work to grow. In a September 1866 report, published while a cholera epidemic swept through London, William reported three sites at which the Mission held seventeen open-air and twenty indoor meetings a week. The mission grew by adding stations and members, absorbing other missions, and renting larger halls.[4]

A "Biblewoman," Eliza Collingridge, became William's first paid employee, and James Dowdle became the first paid evangelist. Eliza visited house-to-house, distributed tracts, and led women's Bible study and prayer groups. She also became a forceful preacher, and by 1868, William had assigned her to superintend a station. She was the first woman to hold such a post. Six years later, another woman, Annie Davis, became the first woman to lead a mission station full-time.

The need to acquire more halls and meeting places was unrelenting. It was time for a headquarters building and a systematic organization, a council of gentlemen to advise William and provide financial backing. That happened in 1867.

The need for a headquarters building was met when Booth and his supporters were able to purchase the Eastern Star, a burned-out beer house that had been notorious for immorality. Undaunted, the Mission rebuilt it with a bookstore in front and a hall in back. Classes were conducted upstairs; there was a reading room with refreshments, a place for mothers' meetings, Bible classes, and believers' meetings, and a residence for Eliza Collingridge and her husband. It was ideal for a mission operation.

During 1867, William also gathered a council of ten men, known for their philanthropic and religious work. They provided guidance and financial support and produced the Mission's first audited financial report.

The Christian Year Book, 1868, reported that William

Booth was becoming recognized as an expert organizer of religious work among the poor. It also recorded that he was "carrying on evangelistic work on a large scale."

This was no exaggeration. From 1867 to 1870, the number of stations, leaders, and members in the Mission increased substantially, primarily due to the work of lay members. In 1868, for instance, William reported 140 weekly services and a total of 4,000 people seeking salvation since 1865.

By 1869, East London Theatre congregations alone averaged nearly two thousand on Sunday evenings. Lay workers were opening mission stations at Bow Common and Old Ford. Other workers were assuming the financial responsibility for renting rooms to hold meetings.

In spite of this tremendous growth, William continued to have problems finding buildings large enough to permit growth, yet not so expensive to rent that they would become a financial burden. Support for the work continued to come in from many sources—philanthropists, the Evangelisation Society, and other groups and individuals who were in accord with the work that was being accomplished, as well as the Mission's council.

Characteristic of the nature of the work being done, and the people being reached, was an article that appeared about this time in the magazine *The Christian World,* detailing the writer's visit to the Apollo Music Hall. He noted that while on weekdays "the hall is densely crowded by young people of both sexes who amuse themselves by mimicking and listening to the popular comic songs of the day, on Sunday evenings all is changed. The mirrors and gaslamps are as resplendent as ever; the greasy benches are as densely occupied; but the waiters, the orchestra of three performers, and the comic singers have disappeared. . . . Instead of roaring noisy choruses of popular songs, those present devoutly raise their voices in gladsome notes of praise to their Maker. . .even the unwashed, grimy-looking idlers who lounge at the public house bar appear somewhat touched. They certainly seem very uncomfortable. They slowly put down their pipes, leave off drinking their beer, and either enter the hall from the bar or else betake themselves to the tap room."

The Apollo proprietor lost his license—the weekday character of the place being so bad—and the building was bought out. The Mission was shut out when the place was closed. But not for long! William Booth, with George White accompanying him, went to the brewery office, and in the end the proprietors let the Mission use the hall free of charge for weekdays as well as Sundays. The Mission continued to use the facility until the end of 1875.

Free breakfasts for the poor on Sunday mornings were another means the Mission used to reach people. The Cambridge Music Hall was the site for such a breakfast where a thousand residents of the neighborhood gathered. At the East London Theatre, between eight hundred and nine hundred persons sat down to such a breakfast. The *Morning Advertiser* in reporting on this stated that, "The congregation. . .had come from the back slums, from fetid courts and alleys, from the casual wards, from the registered lodging houses, from sleep on doorsteps and in railway arches. . .a mixed multitude; . . . denizens of distant countries were there. . .every variety of feature. . .all were thinly clad, the bulk in rags and tatters."

There were many remarkable conversions resulting from these theater breakfasts.

Close cooperative efforts between the organization of the Friends and the Mission existed in which they expressed "a feeling of deep concern for the teeming multitudes of the vast city with desires for their temporal and spiritual good." In speaking at one of the Friends' meetings, William Booth urged that more Christians "go and lay their hands upon them [the poor] and let them feel the touch of warm sympathy. Christian men, come and lay hands on them, giving us one, two, or three days a week; come and do the work altogether; there is an open door! Your friends go to China—is not a poor English brother or sister as worthy of your kindness as a poor Chinese? Come, and God will richly repay you here and in the world to come!"

Neglect of the needs of the poor in London greatly disturbed William Booth, and he felt constrained at every turn to help and save them.

twelve

As the 1860s came to a close, William and Catherine had many reasons to be encouraged in their work, but they also carried personal sorrows. On the ministry front, the Mission continued to grow. Catherine was serving as editor of the Mission's publication *The Christian Mission Magazine,* in which she published many of her own articles. Her preaching continued in areas out side London's East End, and as a result people asked for branches of the Mission to be established outside East London.

As gifts and funding gradually increased, it became possible for a place called the People's Market on Whitechapel Road to be acquired and transformed into a People's Mission Hall. Where before they had been renters, now they would be owners. (It was the first in what was to become an incredible number of such places worldwide.) Instead of dreary comfortless surroundings, William envisioned a meeting place where "a rich harvest of souls" could take place and where those who came to the penitent's form could be dealt with in a way that would insure proper follow-up. In this place they were to go on to develop an impressive home mission program which emphasized "outdoor relief," that is, handouts of food and clothing, soup kitchens and free teas, maternal societies, a Bible woman's door-to-door survey of spiritual and physical needs, and assistance programs to those who were so in need.

More than one helper had pointed out to the Booths what a mockery it was to talk about people's souls while their bodies were perishing with hunger. Booth was no man to console empty bellies with promises of spiritual bliss. He saw. He listened. He knew Christ's command, "Give ye them to eat." His Food for the Million Shops and other such endeavors flourished.

They soon found themselves immersed in finding work for the unemployed and assisting immigrants. While saving souls was always William's and Catherine's primary focus, the "soup, soap, and salvation" idea had kicked in, and there was nothing that could be done to stem the tide. The needy were everywhere, and the Booths could not turn a blind eye to the daily struggles the poor of England faced.

But William and Catherine confronted their own struggles, as well. During 1869, Catherine's beloved mother feel ill with breast cancer. Catherine moved her mother next door to the Booths' home so that she could care for her during her last days. On December 16, Mrs. Mumford momentarily regained consciousness, exclaimed, "Kate!—Jesus!" and died.[1]

While Catherine withdrew from active ministry to grieve the loss of her mother, her seclusion did not last long. In early 1870, William became so ill that Catherine had to fulfill many of his responsibilities, including preaching and administration. Once he recovered, young Bramwell caught rheumatic fever, and then Emma injured her hand.

And while the work of the Mission continued to grow, some branches decided to break off and become independent. This was a blow to both William and Catherine, who, although quite independent themselves, did not appreciate that same quality in others.

The men and women who chose to associate themselves with the work and were willing to tolerate the Booths' leadership style (which even their friends admitted could be autocratic at times) left their own indelible marks.

William's genius conceived of the idea that converts were saved to serve. Whenever it was possible, their help was enlisted in the Mission's work. Many of these people had literally been lifted from the gutter, yet it was their testimonies to God's love and grace that proved most compelling to drunkards, thieves, and others considered by society as unsalvageable.

It was not only these converts who became workers. Philanthropists and well-educated Christians of some means and wide influence were attracted to the movement, leading hundreds, even thousands, to Christ.

There was ongoing help and interest from other

mission organizations and some churches. Links were forged that held promise and brought about great things in the future. Many converts improved their lot in life with the aid of the Mission and later emigrated to all parts of the world, carrying with them the gospel message.

The Mission was also influenced by a spirit of militarism in the world at large. The public had been inundated with reports of the American Civil War in the early 1860s, followed by the Russo-Turkish War. The stirring processional hymn "Onward, Christian Soldiers" was released by the Reverend Sabine Baring-Gould in 1865, the same year that the Booths began their work in East London, and it became a popular tune used by the Mission's workers. Fighting hymns in general were greatly used. By 1872, reports flooding into Booth's Whitechapel Road headquarters were full of military terminology. The people's preoccupation with wars throughout Europe and the question of whether war was again coming to the British was reflected in the symbolic use the leaders of the Christian Mission made of military terminology. Phrases such as "siege operations" against the devil and "toe-to-toe with the enemy" became common.

One of the most militant men to play a major role in the work was "Fiery Elijah" Cadman, from Coventry, Warwickshire. At age six, he answered a chimney sweep's advertisement: "Wanted—Small Boys for Narrow Flues." At 4:00 A.M. every day, the little boy would go to work. With a mask over his face and a scraper in his hands, he would loosen the soot in fireplaces. When he fell, grazing his little limbs red-raw, his wounds were bathed in a saline solution to heal and harden them.

From infancy, Fiery Elijah was hardly ever sober. As a teenager he went to Rugby and headed a street gang called the Rugby Roughs. Later, as a fearless bantamweight, he opened a boxing saloon in a tavern to stage public exhibitions. Conversion came when he and a friend, as a post-Christmas diversion, attended the last public hanging ever held outside Warwick jail. As the body dropped, Cadman's friend said, "That's what you'll come to, Elijah, one day."

A small but sturdy eighteen-year-old, with short legs and a loud and forceful voice, Elijah was immediately overcome by a sense of his past sins. In a typically impulsive gesture, he smashed his own boxing saloon, swore off tobacco and liquor, and proclaimed that now he would fight as hard for God as ever he had fought for the devil. He started out as a Methodist lay preacher, attracting large crowds by ringing a huge handbell and billing himself as "The Saved Sweep from Rugby."

Still Elijah craved an outlet for his brimming energies, and in August 1876, after hearing William Booth preach, he volunteered—and was accepted—as a Christian Mission evangelist. "By the help of God," he vowed, "I'm going to help wake up the churches and chapels." They weren't empty words.

William Booth chose his workers shrewdly. It was stated that more than any of his early workers, Elijah Cadman could rock a crowd on its heels as surely as ever he had rocked his adversaries in the prize ring. Within weeks of becoming a part of the Mission, Elijah sent out a stirring call for two thousand men and women to join "The Hallelujah Army" in the fight against the devil's kingdom. He arranged for mammoth posters declaring: "WAR! WAR IN WHITBY! THE HALLELUJAH ARMY, FIGHTING FOR GOD!" On his own initiative, he then took another daring step. His advance billing pronounced William "General of the Hallelujah Army."

Suddenly, the little man got cold feet! *Oh my! What if the General didn't like it?* So Elijah hid the poster in his house. William stayed at Elijah's house and spotted the poster. "Cadman, I must commend you on your enterprise," he said.

For once, Fiery Elijah was speechless.

"I want you to send a copy to George Railton at Whitechapel Headquarters," William instructed.[2]

Elijah's campaign in Whitby won three thousand followers. He was a worker-leader to be reckoned with. William was thankful to have him as part of the work. Fiery Elijah was the first in the Mission to dramatize the struggle against Satan as war. He referred to himself and his companions as troops and as an army. He was the first worker to call himself captain, as well as the first to advertise William as the general.

Later, as the Christian Mission became The Salvation Army, the branch missions in various cities were called corps, uniforms were designed, ranks and titles were made standard, and a whole vocabulary of military terms came into use.[3]

The George Railton who was at headquarters when this story took place was to prove to be the most valued aide in this era, a man destined to serve the cause unfailingly for forty-eight years.

Railton came to William as a result of reading the

six-penny pamphlet *How to Reach the Masses with the Gospel.* "These are the people for me," George exclaimed, his eyes afire. He was, at the time, a part-time Methodist Mission worker at Middlesbrough, Yorkshire. He came on board the Christian Mission in March 1873 as William's private secretary. He agreed to lodge temporarily with the family and remained a beloved member of the household for eleven eventful years. He was in sympathy with Catherine Booth, who shared his belief in hard work and self-denial. George Railton was indefatigable from the first. He was indifferent to hardship. More than anything, George was an organizer who was zealous in his commitment to the cause.

It was Railton who in 1878 confronted William about the need to dispense with what he called the "long-winded process of government by conference."

"When we came to be a part of the Mission, we hadn't bargained with handing over our lives to a committee's deliberations," he said. "We gave up our lives to work under *you* and those you appoint."

William found himself in a quandary. He himself wasn't a lover of committees. He was known to say, "If there had been committee meetings in the days of Moses, the children of Israel would never have got across the Red Sea." But he'd had eleven years of abiding by a committee's rules and decisions, ever since the council of ten men had been established in 1867.

Catherine challenged him: "Where is it all leading? Are we a religious body or are we an appendix to the churches?"

William, perplexed, could only respond: "Kate, I don't want to found a new sect."

123

Early one morning in May 1878, Bramwell Booth and George Railton were summoned to William's bedroom to compare notes and receive instructions for the day's work. This was a customary meeting. Although William was recovering from the flu, he was able to meet with the men. Together they scanned the proofs of a pink eight-page folder that comprised the Mission's annual report. On the front were the words:

THE CHRISTIAN MISSION
Under the superintendence
Of the Reverend William Booth is
A VOLUNTEER ARMY
Recruited from amongst the multitudes who
are without God and without hope in the world.

Bramwell, who was twenty-two at the time, objected to the wording: "Volunteer!" he shouted. "Hey, I'm not a volunteer. I'm a regular or nothing! We feel we *must* do what we do, and we are *always* on duty."

His words stopped William cold. His eyes were fixed on his son. Abruptly, he leaned over George Railton's shoulder and, taking the pen from his hand, with a decisive movement crossed through the word *volunteer* and substituted the word *Salvation*.

The three men looked at each other. They knew that something very definitive and special was happening. The three leaders of the Christian Mission, united in spirit, gave the organization a new name, wholly and unmistakably descriptive of its purposes and character. The appropriateness of this action has never been questioned.

On Wednesday, August 7, 1878, during the last morning session of the Christian Mission's annual Whitechapel conference, William summoned the determination for what he had to do. He moved a resolution to scrap the Mission's Deed Poll and substitute another. Control of all Mission property in Britain or any other country was now vested in him as general superintendent or in his nominee —as also was the power and duty to appoint his successor. Power to change or modify this deed was withdrawn. No alteration was possible without recourse to Parliament.

The resolution was prompted by a radical urge to get things done without action being held up by endless committee meetings, and the motion carried by a three-fourths majority.[4]

The sessions of the congress in that particular year found William Booth impressing upon all the need for receiving power from God in order that the great work of the past might be far exceeded in the future. There was much jubilation among the delegates as they shared "War Memories" and encouraged each other in the work.

It was at this session that William declared his vision for The Salvation Army: "The distinguishing features are to be (1) authority, (2) obedience, (3) the adapted employment of everyone's ability, (4) the training of everyone to the utmost, and (5) the combined action of all.

"Through such a system, although mostly unknown in the religious world, we can best accomplish our purposes. Why should it not be possible to raise an army of crusaders for the salvation of souls as it once had been to raise armies for the recovery of a sepulchre?"

The process by which the Christian Mission adopted

a military form of government and thus prepared itself for transformation into The Salvation Army was considered a truly democratic process.

Former Commissioner Thomas B. Coombs, who was at the 1878 Congress, wrote in 1935: "The real and inner meaning of the change was that the Movement was experiencing growing pains. . . . It could not wait for committee meetings which often meant long and meaningless speeches, but had to get on with the real work which was in the hands of men and women at the front. It was a radical Salvation urge of 'up and at it!' I do not think there was any serious opposition. . .older men, who came from different Methodist denominations, were accustomed to conferences and voting—and they would be sure to have some remnants of the 'old clothing' with them. If there were any of the rank and file who objected, it was from the same cause, and a passing affair. In the main, everybody was for it. The great mass was swallowed up with the work they had in hand."[5]

William Booth, speaking at St. James Hall, London, in 1881, summed up the process which resulted in the creation of The Salvation Army with these words: "We tried, for eleven years, various methods. We tried many plans. . . . Gradually the Movement took more of the military form, and finding, as we looked upon it, some four years ago, that God in His good providence had led us unwittingly, so to speak, to make an army, we called it an army, and seeing that it was an army organized for the deliverance of mankind from sin and the power of the devil, we called it an army of deliverance; an army of salvation—The Salvation Army."

thirteen

Although General William Booth used uneducated men and women—very often people with little or no appreciation for culture—he never assumed that education wasn't important. When the ranks of the Army and the work began to increase dramatically, and larger numbers of officers were necessary, the Booths set aside a son and two daughters to train the cadets.

Today, the operations of The Salvation Army are supervised by trained, commissioned officers. They proclaim the gospel and serve as administrators, teachers, social workers, counselors, youth leaders, and musicians. But all this was to develop over a period of time.

As fast as possible, William was training men and women to go out into the field, but it was uphill work. Prior to 1880, when he moved his family into a sixteen-room house in the northeast corner of Clapton Common, East London, no training facilities had even existed. But after the move, the Gore Road house was fitted up to take thirty women cadets, trained under William and Catherine's daughter Emma.

A year later, the general's second son, tall fiery Ballington, was given charge of a training home for men at Devonshire House in Hackney. The rigors of the routine at Devonshire House were spartan. It was practical from first to last. Recruits had to face up to bad eggs being thrown at them and filthy abuse in open-air meetings; then they learned how to wash the wasted bodies of the sick and comb their matted hair. High-flown theology had no part in their training. To qualify for what lay ahead of them, these volunteers needed both stamina *and* faith.

In November 1881, William raised fifteen thousand pounds to buy the London Orphan Asylum, Clapton, which was, at best, a vast chilly barracks girdled by high brick walls. It became the facility to train cadets and men officers, under the direction of Ballington, who was twenty-three years old. Ballington had been eight years old when his father began the work of the Christian Mission, so, like the other Booth children, he grew up with the principles that shaped The Salvation Army. He was an exceptionally gifted young man whose entire education was aimed at making him an evangelist for the Army. Possessing an extraordinary voice and his father's powers of oratory, his popularity knew no bounds among the Salvationists themselves, as well as among the general public. Trainees under his charge were motivated and inspired by his example and work among them.

Grants to keep the work going were now even more dependent on the whims of philanthropists. One wealthy

Methodist, Dr. James Wood, a Lancashire lawyer, wouldn't give more than one hundred pounds until he had personally attended a Whitechapel meeting and sat among the converts. There he had a close-up view of these working men and women, and he noticed that all of them had washed their necks and ears. "General," he later enthused, "yours is a work of practical godliness. I shall give you one thousand pounds."

Later, when Ballington was sent to a new field of work, his sister Evangeline (Eva) Booth was assigned director of what was then called the International Training College at Clapton, a post she held for four years. She had gone into full-time service for the Army at the age of seventeen. She was striking in appearance, tall—five feet, ten inches—and slender, with a wealth of flowing auburn hair, and a lovely face dominated by deep, flashing eyes. She was an active and physically fit young woman. Over the years, this remarkable young woman was to rise from the lowest rank in The Salvation Army, a sergeant, to commander of The Salvation Army in the United States. Even later she would come to be known as General Evangeline Booth.

In the United States, she was described as "one of God's best gifts to America." During an administration of thirty years she became, for most Americans, the personification of The Salvation Army. But that was not to happen before she demonstrated time after time, in a multiplicity of places and events around the world, her many abilities. She suffered mob violence and police persecution along with other Salvationists in the 1880s, and she came to be used as a troubleshooter—sent whenever a critical battle was in progress. Whether facing severe legal tests or rebellious crowds, the cry would go out, "Send Eva!"

Eva was definitely her father's daughter, displaying a strong personality in her own right. She proved innumerable times that she had both her parents' gift of stirring audiences small and large. As the head of The Salvation Army in the United States, appointed by her father, she received the tributes which, by then, were accruing to the Army. She was received by Presidents Theodore Roosevelt, Taft, Wilson, Harding, Coolidge, Hoover, and Franklin Delano Roosevelt, each of whom endorsed the work of The Salvation Army. Commander Eva Booth was considered one of the eminent speakers of her day and recognized as a leader in the movement for women's suffrage and prohibition legislation. In any list of outstanding American women in the first half of the twentieth century, the name of Evangeline Cory Booth is certain to appear.

Her father William was a man far ahead of his time. He was very cognizant and appreciative of the role of women. It was he who often stated, "Some of my best men are women."

In the *Christian Mission Magazine* (April 1878), William commented on the number of women evangelists then working with the Mission:

> *In externals nothing is more remarkable in the recent progress of the Mission than the great advance of our female ministry. It has sometimes been said that female preachers would be the ruin of the Mission. But on the contrary, it turns out that the prosperity of the work in every respect*

*just appears most preciously at the very times
when female preachers are being allowed the
fullest opportunity.*

*During the past month sisters have been tak-
ing a leading position in the work at no less than
nine out of the thirty-six stations. We have at present twenty married evangelists and sixteen of
the twenty wives have already taken a great part
in the public services.*

Perhaps as much as anything, it was his own love and
gratitude for his wife and what from the outset he observed she was capable of doing that influenced William.
Early on Catherine was affectionately given the title
"Mother of The Salvation Army." Every phase of their
work bears testimony to her influence as the inspirer and
sharer of William Booth's labors and leadership. Certainly
the remarkable strengths of their daughters and daughters-
in-law were influential in determining William's continuing high regard for the role of women.

Many people disagreed with The Salvation Army's
official position that men and women should have equal
roles within the ministry. Some people left the organization because of their objections to this position. But
William and Catherine were not swayed. They were convinced that Scripture held God's sons and daughters in
equal regard, and when William and Catherine believed
something was in accordance with God's will, nothing
would keep them from obeying.

One of the things that the general was fast learning, and

that he then passed on to his officers, was that "it is in the interests of the service [The Salvation Army] to be in the columns of the newspapers as often as possible." He has been inaccurately credited with inventing such eye-catching titles as "The Hallelujah Lassies," describing the women of the Army. Actually, the billing was the brain-child of William Crow, a Newcastle printer, who had been briefed to run off a handbill announcing the arrival of "Two Lady Preachers," Rachel and Louise Agar, on Tyneside. Crow, feeling the announcement lacked punch, called them instead "The Hallelujah Lassies"—a title which shocked William to the core.

Within days, however, results came flooding in to Whitechapel headquarters. Hour after hour brought more telegrams and inquiries, and no building on Tyneside was large enough to accommodate the crowds who came flocking to hear the Hallelujah Lassies. Miners and dock-workers, accustomed to calling their own wives "lassie," were curious and so anxious to hear more about this "strange new religion" that they rushed to come to the meetings. William Booth could hardly have guessed that the phrase would echo around the world, but he did learn an abiding truth from the "Hallelujah Lassies" incident: Any publicity that kept the Army's mission before the public and brought such results was good publicity.

From then on, William's soldiers took his injunction to heart. The officers were totally uninhibited, their methods as varied as what they sometimes wore. One man toured the streets as John the Baptist, barefooted, dressed in a skin hearth rug. East London lasses drew record crowds parading the streets wearing their nightgowns over their uniforms. Lieutenant Kitching, a mild-mannered Quaker who was also a schoolteacher, cheerfully rode into Yorkshire perched on a crimson-draped donkey. To advertise *The War Cry,* he borrowed the schools' dinner bell and jangled it through the streets.

The Army's officers were not merely being sensationalists. Having seen how these "circus-barker tactics" could draw a crowd, they became passionate pleaders for righteousness and reconciliation to God. Bizarre props became commonplace—sometimes officers swept through a town beating frying pans with rolling pins. Someone even made a billboard as high as a three-story house. Most prominent of all the attention-getters was "Happy Eliza" Haynes, a rip-roaring factory girl from William's hometown, Nottingham.

When Eliza found all normal publicity methods falling flat, she marched boldly through the city streets with streamers floating from her unbraided hair and jacket, a placard on her back proclaiming "I am Happy Eliza." Then, to the tune of "Marching through Georgia," she marched at the head of a band of singing ruffians, conducting George Scott Railton's words with a fiddlestick:

Shout aloud Salvation, boys! We'll have another song!
Shout it with a spirit that will start the world along
Sing it as our fathers sang it many million strong,
As they went marching to glory!

Happy Eliza became close to a national figure. She did all sorts of things to call attention to the meetings and gained an enormous following. Was it any wonder she was commissioned a lieutenant? Music hall ditties, dolls, even sweets were named after Eliza Haynes. She had taken to heart the words of Catherine Booth: "I would lead Hallelujah Bands and be a. . .fool in the eyes of the world to save souls!"

The incredibly rapid growth of The Salvation Army called for literature, and so in 1879 William began publishing a magazine which came to be called *The War Cry*. His soldiers needed to be kept abreast of each other's work, and the paper built morale. The paper also provided a source of income for the Army, and served to introduce the Army and its work to the general public. Copies were published monthly, but success and demand changed it to a weekly. Designed to promote conversions and to raise operating funds, it was immensely successful.

William told his soldiers, "Let *The War Cry* go everywhere. Quick!" Eva Booth, at seventeen, was one of the most successful *War Cry* salesgirls. The story is told that as each issue came off the press she would memorize the names of various cities, towns, or countries mentioned in some of the articles and columns, and then, like a hawking newsboy, she would follow a prospective buyer down the street, calling out the list of places in the hope that they would be of special interest.

Both the General and Mrs. Booth were frequent contributors to the magazine, but no one could have envisioned the time when 136 Army periodicals, totaling almost 2 million copies per week, would be a routine international print run. The news columns, in particular, became famous in many different languages in the various countries where The Salvation Army work was being so effectively carried on.

The print ministry of the Army—which included *The War Cry*, a hymnbook, pamphlets, and books by both Booths, *Salvation Army Doctrines,* and *Orders and Regulations*—embodied the aim and spirit of the Booths when they launched The Salvation Army. William Booth could have become a very rich man if he had taken the profits from his literary labors, but he refused. The present-day mission statement expresses what has always been at the heart of the movement:

> *The Salvation Army, an international movement,*
> *is an evangelical part of the universal Christian*
> *Church. Its message is based on the Bible. Its*
> *ministry is motivated by the love of God. Its*
> *mission is to preach the gospel of Jesus Christ*
> *and to meet human needs in His name without*
> *discrimination.*[1]

Catherine Booth designed the first flag used by the Army. It has changed somewhat through the years, but still bears the stamp of its cofounder. Today the flag has a dark blue border around a red rectangle, in the center of which is a yellow star inscribed with The Salvation Army motto, "Blood and Fire." Blue symbolizes the purity of God; the crimson center the atoning Savior; and the yellow star the fire of the Holy Spirit.

The motto was taken, not surprisingly, from the Bible: "And I will shew wonders in the heavens and in the earth, blood, and fire, and pillars of smoke" (Joel 2:30).

William was an insatiable perfectionist, known to say, "This and better will do," when things ran smoothly. So it was that he began to feel that a fighting force should look distinctive. In Victorian days uniforms were to be seen everywhere. It would be two years, however, before William's dream of a standard uniform could become reality.

Catherine also recognized the need for more suitable attire for this volunteer Army. Some wore outfits that were totally unsuitable, if not downright ridiculous. Some officers dressed in what she felt was "too worldly" a fashion. Extremes in taste were reflected in various manners of dress.

The Booths called their family and the volunteer leaders together. Explaining their concerns, Catherine stated, "How would you feel about uniforms?" There was general agreement on the issue, but not all Salvationists took kindly to the proposed change. Even George Railton expressed doubt: "Uniforms might set us apart from the masses." Once William convinced his friend of the usefulness of uniforms, however, Railton became the first man to wear a full Salvation Army uniform.

Still, it took time to bring this about, and the officers improvised as best they could, some even wearing second-hand British Army uniforms of varying styles and periods. The force that had begun as a rabble of dedicated volunteers slowly became a more organized regiment. Some wore postmen's caps with red ribbons or firemen's blue jackets with a do-it-yourself brass *S* on the lapel. Some tore the printed title, *The War Cry,* from the top of their publication and fastened it around their caps or hats.

Catherine finally designed standard uniforms of red

and blue, the colors of the Army—blue serge patrol jackets, worn over crimson guernseys, or fishermen's jerseys. It wasn't until the spring of 1880 that captains—then the highest Army rank—could apply to headquarters for these uniforms.

For women officers there were initially Princess Robes. Then, since hats were important for women to wear in public, Catherine and her daughter Emma collected an assortment of bonnets and closeted themselves in a room, hoping to settle on one that suited them both. "Mother, how do you like this one?" Emma asked, parading in front of her mother.

"No. . .no, that won't do," said the determined Mother of the Army and mother of the child.

"What do you think of this one, Emma?" Catherine asked of her young daughter. It was proving more of a challenge than either had reckoned.

None actually satisfied either of them. Together they settled on a bonnet that seemed the most suitable, and then Catherine summoned a young cadet who, fortunately, was a milliner by trade. Mother and daughter discussed with the young man what they had in mind and, giving him the bonnet selected, instructed him to modify it according to their specifications. The headgear settled on was a black, straw bonnet with broad missile-resistant brim, trimmed with black silk and strings.

Soon the hat became known as the "Hallelujah Bonnet" because the women wearing it, in their enthusiasm, often shouted "Hallelujah!" during services or in discussions with potential converts. Originally the brim of the bonnet was considerably wider than it is today. It was effective in protecting the wearer from ripe tomatoes thrown at them or from beer poured on them by sneering drunks when the girls knelt to pray for sinners on the sawdust floors of Whitechapel saloons.

The bonnet was first worn by twenty-five women officers marching from Hackney to Whitechapel on June 16, 1880, for the silver wedding anniversary celebration of William and Catherine Booth.

The uniforms and bonnets presented a financial problem. Salvationists paid for their uniforms out of their own pockets, and in those pioneer years many couldn't afford to spend a pound for a Princess Robe or a guinea for a captain's outfit. It would be ten years before the Army's tailoring department showed a twelve thousand pound-a-year profit, a sum which, as was the custom, was ploughed back into the fighting fund.

The adoption of uniforms and military titles and the use of military terminology disturbed Queen Victoria. After all, her army was supposed to be the only army in England, and she was its royal commander. She took no direct action to stop the Booths, but William did receive word that the queen opposed his "generalship" and the military aspects of the organization.

In truth, William had never given himself the title of general. When the first printer's proof that gave him that title was handed to him for approval, he scrawled on the proof, "Can't this form be altered? It looks pretentious." But like it or not, the rank that Elijah Cadman had bestowed on William in Whitby was a fixture: William Booth was a general with an army that needed his leadership.

Queen Victoria's antagonism was communicated to the middle and upper classes. Those who disliked William and his methods were pleased that the queen was of their mind. But those who tolerated, or had even encouraged Booth, were not inclined to risk Queen Victoria's displeasure by giving assistance to The Salvation Army. Even the mobs that attacked William and his followers picked up on the queen's attitude, feeling that it gave them a degree of immunity from any serious police action.

Ultimately, however, the queen recognized that The Salvation Army's aims and efforts were commendable, though she never ceased to resent the fact that "General" Booth and his "officers" led an "Army" in her empire! It wasn't until her son, Albert Edward, was crowned King Edward VII in 1901 that the royal attitude changed for the better. King Edward was intensely interested in every cause and movement that would benefit his subjects, and he openly gave his blessing and generous support to The Salvation Army. It was a kingly move which later served to open wide the door for General Booth in the castles and courts not only of England, but of other nations.

Many supporters of the Army who couldn't give money responded to appeals for worn furniture, cast-off clothing, or other possessions which the Army could renovate and use or sell, bringing much-needed revenue. The big Salvation Army trucks rumbling down the streets in towns and cities today picking up people's discards are performing the same service.

The salvage of merchandise was both secondary and essential to the spreading salvage of sinners.[2] Those who had been outcasts of respectable society—many living in unbelievable squalor—and had come to the Lord and experienced spiritual rebirth and salvation because of the work of the Army, now, with the Army's help, were able to begin the uphill climb to clean and decent living. The magnitude of the social services work of the Army is mind-boggling and continues internationally to this day.

The Salvation Army thrived on persecution. New recruits were gathered, new corps were opened, and prominent friends were made as the value of the work became evident.[3]

Not only in Britain were Salvationists ready to court ridicule, but already in the United States, Salvationist emigrants had begun working in their new country and were successfully capturing the attention of the people in America. They had opened fire in Philadelphia and were begging the headquarters in Britain for reinforcements. No Army could reject such love and zeal from troops who had mobilized themselves.

"I need seven 'Hallelujah Lassies' to show America what women inspired by God can do," George Railton said, pressing his claims on Catherine. "It's fertile territory. Help me persuade the general to send me to America."

The general was faced with a major decision. What did God want him to do?

fourteen

T he work of first the Christian Mission and then The Salvation Army moved with such rapidity that more than one supporter asked William Booth, "Where are you going to get your preachers?"

William replied, "We shall get them from the public houses. Men who have felt the fire will be the best men to rescue others, and we shall never fail in getting the right men."

His declaration literally came true, but William never intended to get his preachers exclusively from the public houses. The majority of the leaders of the Christian Mission and then The Salvation Army came from among those who were converted in their youth and consecrated themselves, while still young, to seeking the salvation of others.[1]

Such was certainly the case with one of the emigrants who came to America. The daughter of Amos and Anna

Shirley, Salvation Army officers in Coventry, England, Eliza Shirley was quite familiar with Army ideals.

When Amos Shirley, a silk weaver, decided to emigrate to America in 1878, he left behind his wife, Annie, and only daughter, Eliza, with the idea that when he found suitable work and a place for them to live, he would send for them. That same year, sixteen-year-old Eliza was converted at a Salvation Army meeting. Soon afterward she entered full-time Army work.

Her father, Amos, in the meantime, had successfully found employment as a foreman in a silk factory in a suburb of Philadelphia. He lost no time in sending for his wife and wrote to Eliza that Philadelphia was in great need of the kind of work General Booth was directing in England. "Come with your mother, and the three of us will work together. Come if the Lord wills," he wrote.[2]

Dutifully Eliza prayed, and then with mounting excitement decided to join her father, traveling with her mother. She immediately wrote to General Booth. Although only seventeen, Eliza had already proved to be of great use and blessing to the work in England.

The general stroked his beard as he read Eliza's impassioned plea for his blessing on her decision to join her father. She received an immediate reply reminding her that this was a very serious matter. Had she carefully weighed her call, her precious work, the souls she had already led to the Cross, and what might lie before her? The letter closed with the statement: "We are not prepared to commence operations so far away. . . . But if your letter is the final decision, if you must go, and if you should start a work, start it on the principles of The

Salvation Army, and if it is a success, we may see our way clear to take it over."

William's reluctance to expand to another continent was understandable. The work in England was growing at such a phenomenal pace, there were never enough funds and personnel to go around to meet the existing needs. Eliza was young, bold, and daring, committed to the Lord, full of life and vigor—just what the Army needed. How could he spare even one worker like her? But neither could he stand in her way, knowing as he did how much she relied on God's guidance.

Thus it was that Lieutenant Eliza was allowed to say farewell in the Army's regulation way, but not before the general's youngest son, Herbert, had been sent to visit her. He bore the mission: "Dissuade her if you can, but if she will go, tell her to be careful about the principles of the Army, to start right. She may call it The Salvation Army, and if it succeeds, she is to report."

A wonderful farewell meeting was given in honor of Mother Annie and her daughter Eliza when they sailed for America. In August 1879, the Shirley family was reunited. Eliza, fresh from active ministry as a young Salvation Army officer in England, was welcomed warmly in camp and revival meetings in Philadelphia. She was attractive and zealous, a young warrior in constant demand to speak and sing at holiness and temperance meetings. But the young girl's sympathies were with the "unloved, unreached masses."

Amos Shirley continued as breadwinner for the family, working long hours at the silk factory, while his wife and daughter walked around Philadelphia searching for just the right place to initiate The Salvation Army work in the United States. They had only been in the city a month when they found a one-story, flat-roofed, dilapidated old chair factory. The unplastered walls were black, there was no floor, old chairs were piled in one corner, and an old horse solemnly stared at them from another corner. Patches of blue sky showed plainly through the roof. It wasn't exactly luxury.

Eliza was excited. "Oh, Mother," she exclaimed, "what a wonderful place for the birthplace of The Salvation Army! Jesus was born in a stable and cradled in a manger; this is just right for us."

And so it was that the birthplace of The Salvation Army in America was a stable. The two women could rent the building for three hundred dollars a year. Amos secured the building with a month's rent in advance. In no time they had it cleaned up. Walls were whitewashed, and a platform was built of rough, unplaned lumber. An interested gentleman provided fifty dollars for flooring, and benches which were secured to seat fifty to sixty people.

Scarlet posters were posted conspicuously announcing: "Blood and Fire. The Salvation Army. Two Hallelujah Females will speak and sing for Jesus in the Old Chair Factory at Sixth and Oxford Streets, October 5 at 11 A.M., 3 P.M., and 8 P.M. All are invited."

The term "Hallelujah Females" was used because Mr. Shirley objected to calling his wife a "lassie" and couldn't bring himself to consider his seventeen-year-old daughter a woman. They held an open-air meeting before marching to the factory and were pelted with mud, sticks, stones, rotten eggs, vegetables, and refuse. If the Shirleys had expected a different reception than what William and Catherine Booth and their followers received in England, they must have been surprised.

The incident was just the beginning of persecution that was to grow more fierce. When Mrs. Shirley and her daughter appealed to the mayor of Philadelphia for protection, he told them they were the cause of the disorder and ordered them off the streets. Undaunted, the Shirleys continued open-air meetings and services in the rented building.

One evening a crowd of mischievous boys rolled a tar barrel onto the vacant lot where the open-air meetings were being held and set fire to it. As the flames shot up, the fire department was called out and a crowd gathered. The fire attracted the curious, and from out of the crowd, "a poor besotted, bleary-eyed man, with ragged clothes, tousled hair, and unsteady gait" approached Amos Shirley.

"Is it true what you say? Will your God take the devil's leavings and make something out of them? I'll give Him a chance."

"Reddie" became the first convert of the unofficial Salvation Army in the United States. He was able to reach his old cronies, and night after night, the chair factory filled, and the penitent form was lined with seekers. Money started coming in, and the Shirleys were able to make the old building comfortable for winter. A reporter from the *Philadelphia News* was sent to find out what these "two Hallelujah Females" were doing that could arouse such interest. The upshot of that was an interview with Amos Shirley and a long article about the work in the paper. The Shirleys' Salvation Army was a success. Eliza sent the general the newspaper clipping and reported with much enthusiasm about what was happening.

But Amos Shirley was given an ultimatum: Either give up this Salvation Army nonsense or lose your job. The courageous Englishman came home from work to tell his wife and daughter that he would devote his full time to leading the mission.

Only two months after opening the Salvation Factory, a second corps was established in a hall at Forty-second and Market Streets in West Philadelphia. The date was January 1880. Eliza and a young girl convert took over this meeting place, and the hall was crowed each night. Not long after that, Eliza received word from General Booth that she had been promoted to the rank of captain.

It was at this juncture that George Railton prevailed upon his old friend to allow him to lead additional forces into the United States. The Army's resources—both financial and human—were being taxed to the utmost, and others had tried unsuccessfully to begin a work in the States. A few years earlier (1872–76), James Jermy, a Christian Mission worker, had emigrated to America and begun the Cleveland Christian Mission, and while William sent encouragement, the Mission had not yet evolved a strong enough organizational framework into which the Cleveland, Ohio, work could be drawn. That premature work in America collapsed soon after, and Jermy returned to England.

There were others who, influenced by contact with Booth, found their way to America. In July 1875, the Reverend James E. Irvine came to New Jersey to engage in evangelical work. He had conducted meetings at both the Whitechapel and Chatham stations of the Christian Mission and early in 1875 had married Miss Mary C. Billups, a member of the Booth household. The Billups were unswerving supporters of the Booths, and their daughter entered the Booth household in 1868, becoming one of the most active workers of the East London Christian Mission. But the Jersey City work was premature as well, although Mary and her husband, James Irvine, continued to be staunch supporters of Army work in America.

So it was no wonder that William at first hesitated in sending reinforcements and support for this latest work in America. George Railton pleaded to Catherine: "I feel sure that our own affair in Philadelphia will go with such a sweep that unless we get hold of it, and lead, and go in at full speed at once, I doubt if we should ever be able to get the reins at all. Then it will be a wild affair with no competent direction, and there will be after a while as complete a lull as follows almost all of such things. . . . I do not see why they should not let me go."

When George Railton (with the backing of Catherine) continued to press William, somewhat reluctantly the general agreed to send a detachment to the States. "We were anxious to avoid this a little longer," he stated in his announcement, "seeing how much remains to be done for the millions who remain in utter darkness even in this land of light."

Once he made up his mind, however, William moved quickly, and on February 14, 1880, he appointed George Railton as his first commissioner to broaden the work in

147

America. Railton and a pioneer band of seven women left England aboard the SS *Australia.*

In describing this notable event, Catherine Booth wrote: "We have been in a perfect whirl of excitement. . . . The getting off of dear Railton and the sisters was a scene. Hundreds of people walked in procession. . . . They sang all the way, and omnibuses, wagons, and vehicles of all kinds stopped and lined the roads to see them pass. . . . All the crew and passengers on the ship seemed quite struck, the saloon passengers standing on deck in the rain to listen. . . . It was a grand sight. The women's hats looked capital, being larger, and having a broad crimson band with gold letters. Three of our flags were flying on board, and the enthusiasm of the people seemed to strike with awe even the men who were hauling in the bales. . . . Dear devoted Railton looked well in his uniform, and appeared as happy as an angel. Bless him! I love him as a son. Oh, to win millions for our Savior King! We shall."

The little band arrived at Castle Garden docks in New York City on March 10, 1880. Onlookers must have been surprised to see eight uniformed figures—a young man of rather slight build, very bald in front, black-bearded with a moustache, and seven women—come marching down the gangplank. The detachment of women consisted of Captain Emma Westbrook, thirty-five years old and a veteran of ten-and-a-half years service in The Salvation Army; and Lieutenants Alice Coleman, Rachel Evans, Emma Elizabeth, Florence Morris, Elizabeth Pearson, Clara Price, and Ann Shaw, ranging in age from eighteen to twenty-two.

Gilt letters on the red bands of their black hats

spelled out the words "The Salvation Army." Over their heads a crimson, blue, and gold banner whipped in the raw March breeze, and they were singing hymns.

They were met by the Reverend and Mrs. James Irvine, who took Railton and five of the women to their home in Jersey City for the night. Also at the dock was Amos Shirley from Philadelphia. He returned to Philadelphia with two of the young women lieutenants, Rachel Evans and Clara Price. The next day Mrs. Irvine took her group on a tour of New York City, much of which in those days was crowded into the lower third of narrow Manhattan Island. Brooklyn was mostly farmland; the Bronx a waste of garden patches crisscrossed by dirt roads. Manhattan's towering skyscrapers didn't yet exist.

What struck Railton and his lassies were the statistics of sorrow that New York's wealthy ignored—10,000 children adrift on the streets, panhandling the drunks outside 8,000 saloons. New York had an "East" side, not too unlike London's East End—290,000 people to the square mile living in vile conditions, the poverty and squalor equal to what William and Catherine had encountered in England.

It was the Gilded Age in New York City for those who could afford it—and many could. This Age of Big Business saw the new plutocrats having their teeth set with diamonds or serving cigarettes wrapped in hundred-dollar bills. Crime and vice were unashamed and costly; red lights glowed outside every brothel.

It was a period of great material wealth, and American churches reflected the economic and social changes of the times as well. American Protestantism had largely failed to meet the needs of the urban working class. Just

149

as in London, the poorly dressed working class felt out of place in the churches. It wasn't simply the physical surroundings of these churches but the attitude both of the clergy and their congregations that discouraged the poor from attending church.

Recognizing these conditions had challenged the Shirley family. Once in America and seeing firsthand the situation, George Railton and his courageous band of young women, inspired by a love of Christ and of their fellowmen, joined the battle. They ignored the jibes of critics and marched into the slums to carry the message of salvation to the unreached and unchurched.

"The siege of New York will begin," Railton said, his jaw set with determination. He wasted no time in establishing what he called "Temporary Headquarters" at the Pickwick Lodging House at 130 Liberty Street in the city, and they immediately got to work. Within weeks, a newspaper reported that "none of them can aspirate the letter *h*, but they manage to get on the inside track with a good many hardened sinners, who would listen to some of our pulpit orators with deaf ears."

While there were some critical comments in the press, for the most part The Salvation Army was given a cordial New York reception. In fact, the *Herald,* in an editorial welcome, expressed the hope that The Salvation Army would find "aid, comfort, and allies" and declared: "Its method differs widely from that of any other body of men and women who have given battle to Satan in this city; but the plans of a commander are entitled to respect until someone who has gone successfully over the same ground can be found to criticize them. If by marching through the streets, with colors flying, stopping at corners to sing and exhort, The Salvation Army can persuade any considerable number of men to stop lying, stealing, and cheating and to lead upright lives in the future, no one has the slightest right to complain of the way in which the work is done. Clergymen of various denominations complain frequently that there is a general lack of interest in religious affairs; perhaps if The Salvation Army gains some victories these gentlemen may gain a practical suggestion or two about the way of getting at the nonchurchgoing class."

This favorable publicity helped to make the pioneer Salvationists minor celebrities in New York City. So much interest was aroused that Railton knew they would have to have a sizeable location for their first meeting. He was unsuccessful in getting permission to use Union Square and was unable to secure a hall sufficiently large for an indoor meeting. It was at this point that Harry Hill, attracted by the newspaper publicity, offered to let Railton and his lassies appear in his variety theater as a prelude to the regular performance.

A minister who had offered the use of his church was appalled to learn of Hill's offer and said, "Go there and you will lose your reputation at once and forever. It is the most disreputable den in the country. . .the worst slum in the city!"

"Then that's the place for us," replied Railton.

In less than a month, a flourishing corps had developed in New York City and Newark, New Jersey, and Railton had established his headquarters in Philadelphia.

fifteen

He who loves not women, wine, and song,
Remains a fool his whole life long.

S uch was one of the mottoes that lined the walls of Harry Hill's Variety Theater that cold and foggy night when Railton and The Salvation Army lassies launched their attack against the "kingdom of the devil." They had been out for days up and down the streets of New York, and in particular on each side of Greenwich Street, stopping at the barbershops and barrooms, addressing the customers, and passing out handbills. It pleased Railton that in nearly every instance they were treated with courtesy and respect—quite unlike the treatment they usually met with in England.

The theater was crowded, and people stood three deep in the galleries when the meeting began. Later, reporting to the general, Railton wrote: "As compact a crowd of thoroughly ungodly men and women as could have been hoped for, with perfect liberty to do as we liked whilst we were before them."

The meeting could have been counted a failure, for no one answered the call to the penitent form. Yet out of those initial efforts came the Army's first New York recruit, an old drunken reprobate, James Kemp, better known as "Ash Barrel Jimmy."

Kemp received the moniker because he had once tumbled into an ash barrel headfirst during one of his drunken sprees and was stuck that way until pulled out by a policeman. He was legendary, especially in that part of the city, and news of his conversion punched home as nothing else could have quite done. He couldn't get into the meeting because of the crowd, so he rushed to the Army's headquarters, a converted brothel at 44 Baxter Street, in the heart of the Five Points slum. There he waited until Railton and the lassies found him. This former down-and-outer joined the Army—saved to serve—and serve he did. A captain, Ash Barrel Jimmy served with The Salvation Army until his death fifteen years later.

The Harry Hill Theater meeting dramatically publicized the class of people whom the Army hoped to reach, and as a result, many sympathizers were drawn to the work. New York missions opened doors to them, and well-wishers subscribed enough money so that Railton was able to purchase a fine new hall with a porch for open-air meetings on Seventh Avenue. Prominent every night was the living testimony of "Ash Barrel Jimmy" Kemp.

Railton wasn't able to secure permission to conduct open-air street meetings, even though he petitioned the mayor and the New York City authorities for this. Since this was such an important part of the way The Salvation Army did its work, he made the decision to move his headquarters to Philadelphia. He left behind Captain Emma Westbrook and Lieutenant Alice Coleman to carry on the work in New York.

It was a big assignment, but they, representing the Army, were aggressive in seeking out sinners and battling with Satan in his own strongholds. Those tactics, used today wherever the Army goes, stand as an incredible witness to the faith of those who first went. God has honored those efforts in city after city in the United States and around the world.

Deploying his forces, Railton and the remaining lassies moved on to the city of brotherly love. Two hundred Salvationists with red hatbands rallied to greet him and the women in the old chair factory on Sixth and Oxford Streets. And by May 1880, Railton could cable Booth that his U.S. forces now totaled 16 officers, 40 cadets, and 412 privates. The first year alone saw 1,500 converts. There were twelve corps holding 172 services a week.

Leaving the Philadelphia work in the capable hands of the Shirleys and others, Railton traveled west, always by third class (because there was no fourth), looking for other cities to conquer. In forty-nine days he traveled forty-two hundred miles and delivered eighty addresses. For thirty-one of those nights he slept on straw, railroad benches, and chairs. He wrote that it was "a real soldier's life, and I enjoyed it."

Railton had vowed that he would carry the Army flag

across the Mississippi, and he chose St. Louis, Missouri, as headquarters for what was to be his western campaign. He had informed General Booth that it was imperative that the young Salvation Army lose no time in "going West and growing up with the country."

Railton was full of enthusiasm, if not sometimes impetuous and maybe an impractical crusader. He soon found that street preaching was strictly prohibited. When he hired a hall, the owner abruptly changed his mind and ended the lease—the audience at the first meeting had spat on the floor. No one was willing to lease him another meeting place.

Railton was undaunted. Somehow he had to leave a witness in St. Louis. His solution has become a classic in Salvation Army history. It was November, and a gray, glassy carpet of ice stretched as far as a man could see from the cobblestoned levee across the Mississippi. "It struck me that the authorities could have no power over the iced Mississippi, especially on the Illinois side, so after distributing handbills to most of the men hard at work breaking, cutting, and hauling ice, I went over to the part where the skaters were and began to sing. It was quite a novelty to have a congregation come skating around me at a speed that made it seem certain some would overturn others, but they all seemed too much at home for that, and I spoke plainly to them, urging them to seek pleasures from the Giver of all good and perfect gifts." Imagine it! An evangelist on ice urging a congregation orbiting at full speed to turn and seek God.

In January 1881, Railton was able to begin meetings at Sturgeon Market Hall. He advertised the meeting through handbills distributed at saloons, grocery stores, and on the street corners. "The wisdom of the move was demonstrated by the good number of the ungodly who attended the first meeting," he wrote. On January 15 of that year he launched the first American issue of *The War Cry*.

He stayed in the home of George Parker, "Who took me in," he wrote, "housed and fed me for a whole winter, simply because I was trying to get people saved." Railton's personal expenditures were always kept at an absolute minimum.

But on New Year's Day—the day he began services in the hall—he received a cablegram from General Booth: "Must have you here." Railton was a singular man in that he never complained about the hardships he endured, but the thought of leaving the work that was just getting started, even though he was working alone and against heavy odds, was very difficult. He responded by writing eloquent pleas to stay, arguing that his departure from America would have disastrous effects on so young and weak an organization.

General Booth cabled back just two words: "Come alone."

Herbert Wisbey in *Soldiers Without Swords* explained that it was part of the genius of William Booth that he could remain unmoved by the appeals of this man he so dearly loved. But William knew the needs of his Army better than anyone else, and he put those needs before all things. Railton believed strongly that God would provide for His own and for the work that was begun in the United States. If America was to be saved, the men and women there must do the work. He communicated this to the general and headed home.

William was looking at the work stretching out before the Army—the calls for help from all over the world where saved Salvationists had immigrated, in particular France and Australia—and he recognized that the work desperately required Railton and his organizational capabilities at home, at headquarters. It was no longer possible for the Booths to close their ears to the calls which they were receiving from "the regions beyond." For the first time, William and Catherine acknowledged that The Salvation Army needed to be available internationally.

William also recognized that Catherine's health was weakening. He could not rely as heavily on her as he had in the past. Railton was needed. The loyal soldier returned to the general's side. It was March 1881.

sixteen

T he 1880s were an important period in Salvation Army history. It began a major expansion throughout the world, and the Booths' children began taking leadership roles within the organization.

The work Commissioner Railton had begun in America was continued by Major Thomas E. Moore, forty-two years old. Major Moore was sent from the London and Southern divisions in England to continue establishing a foothold in the United States when Railton was recalled to London. New posts were opened in Pennsylvania, New Jersey, Maryland, New York, Ohio, Michigan, Missouri, West Virginia, and in most of the larger cities of New England. By March 1884, seventy stations were in operation, and two hundred officers followed the flag. And that was just the beginning.

Salvation Army meetings drew large crowds in most American cities—many people were first attracted by the novelty and wanted to satisfy their curiosity, but many curiosity seekers were moved by what they saw. They joined and remained with the Army. The Salvation Army meetings of the 1880s offered release from despairing reality. Those were difficult days for people eking out a miserable existence in the slums of big cities.

Not everyone, however, welcomed the Army. There was a lot of bitterness in the hearts of some people, notably saloon keepers and their habitual customers.

In England, the work progressed with incredible rapidity. The West Enders of London were calling more frequently for Catherine Booth's ministry. "Ah, yes," she responded, "there are broken hearts in the mansions of the rich as truly as in the hovels of the poor." There were no slums to revolutionize there, no ruffians to reform, no vortex of filth and misery to purify. If there was misery, it was alleviated by luxury.

"Since when did money, with all the comforts it can purchase, ever succeed in healing the sorrows of a single soul?" the mother of The Salvation Army asked. In writing to a friend, she stated, "Pray much, dear friend, that God may do a deep and permanent work in this Babylon. . . . He gave me words of fire for them, and they sat spellbound."

As tenderly as Mrs. Booth yearned over repentant sinners, no one could be more scathing in her denunciations of Pharisaical hypocrisy. Writing in another letter to the same friend, she said:

Oh, the hypocrites! How Jesus Christ will expose them in that day! True Pharisees and

159

sons of Pharisees! They for a pretense make long prayers, while they devour widows' houses. . . . God help The Salvation Army to stir up their nests! We are doing it all over the land. . . .

A gentleman was talking to me the other day about the great amount of love there is for the Savior still in the Churches. I said, "Yes, for their idealistic Savior. But suppose Jesus were to come to your chapel as He went about Palestine, with a carpenter's coat on, or as He sat upon the well, all over perspiration and dust with travel, where would your chapel steward put Him to sit?" You should have seen his face! I would have liked Mr. Lee's photographic machine there to have taken it!

She related one of William's trips in which he traveled eight hundred miles, and addressed forty thousand people in eight days (besides holding open-air meetings). "Oh, the stories of grace and salvation! Indescribable!" she exulted. "Heaven must be kept in an uproar of jubilee, if it is true that there is joy there over every one!"

Both William and Catherine spent wearying weeks holding meetings from one end of the country to the other. William was invited to speak to the Wesleyan Conference, which earlier in his evangelism ministry had closed all chapel doors to him. Times had changed, however, and now that William's ministry had gained acceptance, he was "respectfully and kindly received and listened to," as Catherine reported it. Her letters to friends and family are of inestimable value as one seeks to explain the movement of the Army.

"It looks like a miracle! Of course, it is God who does these things for us. I should have thought it much more probable for him [William] to have addressed the House of Lords than those 700 ministers! . . . The Lord still shows Himself strong on behalf of those who serve Him with a perfect heart."

On the occasion of the Booth's silver wedding anniversary in 1880, held at the Whitechapel Hall, friends from all over united with the officers and soldiers of The Salvation Army to celebrate. The most heartwarming feature of the event was when the family rose to their feet, and sang together:

We all belong to Jesus!
Bless the Lord! Bless the Lord!

It is stated in the literature on the Booths that this was a "practical lesson in full consecration [which] was more eloquent than any of the burning addresses given. A little army in itself, it revealed the secret of the success with which the Movement had met. The General and Mrs. Booth had commenced within the narrow circle of their own home the work which had broadened out until it had included within its embrace the entire world."[1]

At times the devil wore a familiar face—respectable Christians, Christian ministers, mayors and members of city councils, and policemen. The Salvationists resisted all urges to cave in to verbal or physical attacks and persecution. Whatever form Satan used to attack the Army's soldiers in their worldwide conquest for Christ, they could not be discredited, and the attacks served only to increase

The Salvation Army's prestige and to widen its influence.

Far afield in Adelaide, Australia, a crucial need for help presented itself. Two men, both converts—John Gore, a milkman, and Edward Saunders, a builder from Bradford —had formed a corps and begun holding open-air and indoor meetings. They sent an appeal to the London head-quarters for help. The immediate decision was made to send Captain and Mrs. Sutherland in January 1881 to join and lead the original pioneers, and every nook and corner of Australian soil was to feel the impact of the Salvationist work. Five years later, the Booth's second son, Ballington, married Maud Charlesworth. They were sent to Australia, where he served as commander; a year later he was com-missioned National Commander USA, and they came to America. Later he was to resign and found the Volunteers of America.

Shortly after the Sutherlands left for Australia, George Railton returned to England from America and immedi-ately plunged into the work of the Army at the general's side. But departures were becoming all too common in the Booth family. That same year, William and Catherine's eldest daughter, the determined, twenty-three-year-old, fair-haired Kate, was sent by the Army to "open fire" in France.

Describing her feelings about Kate's leaving, Catherine wrote to a friend: "I realized as never before dear Katie's going, and felt unutterable things. The papers I read on the state of society in Paris make me shudder, and I see all the dangers to which our darling will be exposed! But, oh, the joy and honor of giving her to be a savior to those dark, sin-stricken masses! Heaven will reveal. Pray for her."[2]

On the occasion of Kate's departure, a farewell was held at St. James Hall and was described as "one of the most enthusiastic and affecting demonstrations that had as yet been held in the history of The Salvation Army."

As she rose to speak, Catherine was obviously deeply touched: "My confidence in God is as strong for France as it has been, and is yet, for England. I believe that the gospel of the Lord Jesus Christ, preached with the Holy Ghost sent down from Heaven, will be as effectual in shaking, convincing, and saving French souls as it has been, and is, in saving English souls. All our confidence is in the Holy Spirit. We should not be so foolish as to send so frail an instrument to that vast and needy country if we thought it depended on human might or power. It is because we know that it depends upon the Divine Spirit, and because we believe that our dear child is thoroughly and fully consecrated to God, and is casting herself upon Him for strength, holding fast to the Divine promise that He will be her sufficiency, that we dare to believe that God will show Himself mighty on her behalf. . .and thus accomplish great and marvelous results in that nation, giving us to see thousands of souls gathered to Himself."

It was a never-to-be-forgotten scene as Catherine presented the Army flag to her daughter and the little band of young women-warriors who accompanied her, with these words: "My dear child and my dear young friends, I consider it an honor, in the name of our Divine Commander-in-Chief, and in the name of the general of this Army, to present you with this flag, as an emblem of the office and position you sustain, and I pray that God may give you grace to uphold the truths which this banner represents, and establish on a permanent and solid basis, The Salvation Army in France. Oh, that He may give you grace to carry it into the slums and alleys, wherever there are lost and perishing souls, and to preach under its shadow the everlasting gospel of the Lord Jesus Christ, so that through your instrumentality thousands may be won from darkness, infidelity, and vice, to Him, their Lord and their God. And in all hours of darkness and trial, oh, may He encompass you in His arms of grace and strength, and fill your soul with His love and peace; and may you begin such a work as shall roll on to generations to come, and ultimately sweep hundreds of thousands into the Kingdom of God! Amen."

It was another landmark in the onward march of The Salvation Army. Kate and her faithful group of young women faced unbelievable opposition but gained the respect of raucous crowds. The French people gave her the name "La Marechale." In 1887, she married Arthur Clibborn, her chief secretary in France. In 1896, Commissioner and Mrs. Booth-Clibborn took command of Holland, with Belgium as a province.

Change continued to mark the Booth family. On October 12, 1882, about a year after Kate left for France, William Bramwell Booth, the eldest son, married Florence Eleanor Soper, an attractive young women, whose father, a doctor in Plymouth, had strenuously opposed her joining The Salvation Army. She had, however, overcome his opposition and had been chief of staff to Kate in France.

At Bramwell and Florence's wedding, both William and Catherine spoke. Catherine paid tribute to her own marriage by saying that "the highest happiness I can wish to my beloved children is that they may realize as thorough a union of heart and mind, and as much blessing in their married life, as the Lord has vouchsafed to us in ours."[3]

The marriage rites were celebrated at Congress Hall, Clapton, by General Booth, who was beginning to see that marriages among his solders were becoming frequent. As a result, the Booths had drawn up "Articles of Marriage which Soldiers Must Agree to before the General Will Marry Them." Considering the long engagement and the beautiful marriage the general and his lady enjoyed, the Booths were certainly qualified to write such a document.

The popularity and ability of Bramwell and his bride was evident. It was understood that he was to be his father's successor; it was destined and unquestioned. He was administratively more capable than anyone else in the Army to assume this responsibility at some future time. Father and son had worked in such intimacy that, although they had different gifts, their minds were remarkably attuned. Bramwell Booth was not only an organizer and a detail-oriented man, he also possessed the fiery piety of his father and the quiet fervor of his mother.

The Booths' third son, Herbert, was also becoming part of The Salvation Army structure. In 1884, he was principal at the International Training School at Clapton, and by 1889, he had been placed in command of the Army throughout the British Isles. In 1890, he married Captain Cornelie Schoch, daughter of a Dutch officer, and was commissioned to Canada in 1892 and sent to Australia in 1896. Herbert was the most talented musician of the Booth children. Though very capable, he frequently rebelled against the authority of his father and held some resentments toward his brother Bramwell, as well. In 1902, he and his wife sent the general a "brokenhearted resignation," and he began a career as an international freelance evangelist.

Change not only marked William and Catherine's family, but it marked The Salvation Army as well. The success of the Army's first ventures into other nations encouraged William and Catherine to extend their efforts to other lands, irrespective of languages and governments. They recognized that in doing this, certain aspects of their work—its rules and regulations—would require adaptations to fit the customs and laws of each country. But they also believed that the main principles they had established were suitable to the whole human race, regardless of local customs.

In 1882, the same year that Bramwell was married, the Army experienced much growth in these international efforts. In Canada, two Salvationist pioneers began work on their own initiative. A handful of earnest enthusiasts entered Switzerland with the gospel message as well. William had assumed that Switzerland would be open to Protestant teachings, but workers in that nation encountered the most bitter, persistent opposition the Army had ever faced. The soldiers refused to give up, even though it meant imprisonment.

One of those imprisoned was Kate Booth, on leave from France. In a letter to her daughter at that time, Catherine Booth wrote: "My darling child, hold on to God, the living God, and don't doubt for one moment but that if He permits the worst to happen He will cause it to work for the spread of salvation to the ends of the earth. . . . Fear not;

be strong and very courageous, for He is with you."[4]

No child of William and Catherine Booth ever shirked a challenge—and there were many of them for these amazing sons and daughters. Kate was no exception. For twelve days she was a prisoner in the cold medieval jail of Neuchatel, Switzerland. Mice scurried on the damp stone floor; the metallic odor of bad plumbing tainted the air. Afflicted like her mother with spinal trouble, she was often in pain. Her father wrote, "Your health is of more importance to me than all Switzerland." But it took more than jail to daunt this spirited young woman, and in the end, it was her stirring appeal to the magistrates and the jury, which led to the acquittal of the Salvationists.

As fast as they could, William and Commander Railton marshaled forces to Germany, Sweden, Holland, Denmark, Zululand, Norway, Belgium, New Zealand, and South Africa.

Then there was India. No one was better qualified to lead the salvation war into that country than Major Frederick St. George de Lautour Tucker, the powerful civil servant who had renounced all to join The Salvation Army. He was grandson of a chairman of the East India Company and son of a judge in India. It was his work in India and the piety and faith he and his soldiers demonstrated that established The Salvation Army in that country on an unshakable foundation and made it an internationally respected missionary enterprise.

Tucker married the Booths' beloved daughter Emma, on April 10, 1888. Upon their marriage he was appointed a commissioner, and Emma a consul. Together they pioneered work in India until 1896, leaving there when the climate proved too much for Emma's health. They were appointed to work in the United States and came to that work at a critical time, just after Ballington Booth and his wife, Maud, left The Salvation Army.

At the marriage of Frederick and Emma, as she did at the marriages of her other children, Catherine Booth spoke movingly of what her daughter meant to her:

When the contemplation of this union was first put before me I confess I found more of the mother left in me than I had imagined. I thought the mother was almost swallowed up in the soldier. I found, however, that there was much of the mother left. There was a great deal of that natural clinging to my precious child, who has been to me more than a daughter; who in time of sickness, and during the absence of her beloved father, and in seasons of family affliction has been to me as a husband and friend. When this marriage came before me, and I saw at a glance what it involved, and as I thought of her value to the War in this country, and especially to those who are so dear to me and to my principles—our female officers all over the world—I staggered. The first impulse was to resist, and say, "No! it cannot be." Then I remembered: "But she is not yours; you gave her at her birth, and you have given her ever since. You have kept her on the altar, and now God wants to go a step in advance of your notions of what you think will be for her physical well-being. Are you going to draw back?" I looked up

to Heaven, and said: "No, Lord; she is Thine,
whatever it may cost, Thou shalt have her for this
particular service, if Thou dost want her."[5]

Emma's light had shone uniquely in the family home. She was considered almost indispensable. From childhood she had been the counselor and burden-bearer, or rather burden-remover, of the family. In 1888, when Emma married, Catherine knew she had breast cancer. Certainly Catherine was wondering, *How will I ever get through this without my Emma?*

Known after his marriage to Emma as Frederick Booth-Tucker (each of the Booths' sons-in-law adopted the famous Booth name to use in hyphenated form with their own), he and his wife were greatly used for eight years in pioneering American hostels for men and rescue homes for women, beginning in New York City, and spreading throughout the United States. They utilized the Army Farm Colony work for the urban poor devised by General Booth and explained in his book *In Darkest England and the Way Out.* They threw themselves into enormous salvage operations, prison work, youth work, and in various innovative ways to supplement the Army's resources and minister.

When the couple's work in the United States ended with Emma's death, her sister Evangeline (Eva) Booth picked up the leadership responsibilities. She had been appointed by her father to be territorial commissioner of Canada in 1896, where she had succeeded her brother Commandant Herbert Booth. She had been instrumental in opening up the Klondike for Salvationist work. To

those miners who pegged out claims for their own enrich-
ment in the rocks and soil and ice, she presented the
claim of God on their lives. It was while returning from
this work that she learned of the tragic death of her sister.

Unknowingly, in 1904, the general bestowed upon
The Salvation Army in the United States its most colorful,
controversial, exciting, and certainly its most durable commander. She proved to be an exceptionally complicated
woman. She had always been given wide latitude by her
father in their hectic household, allowed—even encouraged
—to abandon herself to her strong, inherited dramatic im-
pulses. She was thirty-nine when she was given the enormous responsibility in the States. Although she had several
offers of marriage, she chose to remain single. She adopted
four children: Dot, Jai, Pearl, and Willie.

Evangeline was given the title of commander when
she accepted the post in the United States, and she was
known by that title for thirty years. Her sincerity and
judgment were tested by every kind of situation in the
American melting pot. This vibrant, red-haired daughter
of William and Catherine was heard by all who could
crowd into the biggest halls of the land, and her audiences included the leaders of the United States and other
nations. She drew men and women from the White
House, the Supreme Court, the Embassies, and Congress.
Not only was she heard, but there was a growing respect
for the work of The Salvation Army as a result. The eloquence of Evangeline Booth became legendary.

Commander Booth was also very compassionate,
thoughtful, full of little kindnesses, genuinely sympathetic with the poor and lonely in their sufferings, and a

dedicated, fearless evangelical. A clever administrator, well-informed, decisive, with a good eye for details, she gave her subordinates considerable latitude. She was particularly adept at raising funds for the many needs of the growing Army. Edward H. McKinley in *Marching To Glory* concludes his description of her by stating, "Take her for what she was in fact and in fancy; Eva Booth was a phenomenon of historic proportions."[6]

The Booths' youngest daughter, Lucy Milward, followed the family tradition and entered Army work at an early age. At age sixteen she left with the Booth-Tuckers for India. In 1894, she married a Swedish officer, Colonel Emmanuel Booth-Hellberg. They jointly commanded the Indian Territory until 1896. Two years later they were sent to France and Switzerland (1896–1904). There were four years of sick furlough, followed by work in Denmark (1910–19), Norway (1919–28), and South America (1929–34).

William and Catherine's other daughter Marian had physical and developmental problems that left her unable to do the regular work of The Salvation Army. She never married, remained at home, was given the permanent rank of captain, and lived to be seventy-two.

While three of the Booth children left the work of the Army—painful decisions for all involved—each remained in Christian work. For the Booth family it was "Onward Christian Soldiers" all the way. There were forty-one grandchildren, two of whom died in infancy. Many of these grandchildren carried on the work of their parents and grandparents in The Salvation Army, and the influence of this remarkable family can be felt in the Army to this day.

seventeen

Catherine Booth, arguably the most famous woman preacher of her day, was never ordained. She never held a rank as an officer in the Salvation Army, other than the honorary title of "Mother of The Salvation Army." She helped design The Salvation Army uniform and shape both Army doctrine and some of the startling methods used by the Salvationists. But her greatest doctrinal and practical influence was in the matter of women in ministry, and Catherine Booth was mentor to hundreds of these women.

Women in the Christian Mission and later The Salvation Army saw Catherine Booth as one who fearlessly and consistently took up the cause of women in ministry, not in spite of the gospel but because of it. She was the product, in many ways, of the leveling influence of the great revivalism of the nineteenth century in which salvation was available to women as well as to men, and preaching this good news was the responsibility of women and men alike.[1]

She was always open to the leading of the Holy Spirit and relied on His empowerment to sustain her in her work as wife and mother and in the ministry God entrusted to her.

Her speaking ministry continued throughout most of her life, and wherever she went, thousands attended, with thousands more being turned away. She found herself defending the Army, as well as carefully explaining the means and methods being used to win the world for Christ.

Among the many influential supporters of the Booths' ministry was W. T. Stead, a journalist who also became an invaluable friend and ally of the Army and its founders. He was of inestimable assistance to Catherine in the Maiden Tribute Campaign, a national purity crusade waged between 1883 and 1885 to have the legal age of consent for girls raised from twelve to sixteen.

Out of these exhausting efforts the Women's Social Services work developed, becoming one of the largest rescue organizations in Victorian and Edwardian Britain. It had responsibility for the Army's work with children, prostitutes, and homeless or alcoholic women. Later the ministry was expanded to include unmarried mothers.

Stead also assisted William with the writing of his book *In Darkest England and the Way Out* which was published after Catherine's death.

In February 1888, shortly after returning from meetings at the Free Trade Hall in Manchester and the Colston Hall in Bristol, where both William and Catherine preached, Catherine received fearful news from her physician, Sir James Paget. During intervals of the two-day revival meeting at Bristol, Catherine had told her son Bramwell of a small painful swelling in her left breast. Startled, Bramwell urged his mother to seek the best medical advice without delay, which she had done. The doctor spoke the painful truth: The swelling was a malignant cancer and he urged immediate surgery.

The primitive surgery of those days often only prolonged a patient's suffering. Catherine's own mother had died a lingering and terribly painful death from breast cancer. Facing her own illness, Catherine asked Sir James what her life expectancy would be if the growth went unchecked and she elected not to have surgery. The physician told her two years at the most.

Thus it was that William Booth, who had been waiting nervously for his wife's return that February day, saw the cab swing into their graveled drive. He was due to leave on a whirlwind tour of Holland within the hour. He ran down the steps to greet Catherine. Then he saw that she had been crying. He embraced her and, arms around her shoulders, led her into the drawing room. There he heard the dreadful news.

As Catherine knelt beside him, having finished relating what the doctor had said, she confessed her secret worry: "Do you know what was my first thought? That I should not be here to nurse you at your last hour." William sat stunned and speechless, his hands stroking her hair, gently wiping away her tears. His mind was in a turmoil. "I cannot leave you now; I will not."

"Yes, oh, yes, you must," Catherine protested. "They are waiting for you at the Amsterdam meetings."

En route to the Charring Cross Station, William halted the cab at Queen Victoria Street to break the news to his son. "Bramwell, get her to other surgeons at once. Consult with Sir James. We must have more than one opinion."

William did go to Amsterdam but only stayed for two meetings, canceling the rest. After so many years of remarkable marriage, he found himself helpless to do anything to ease the pain of the woman he so dearly loved and with whom he had shared so much.

Meanwhile, the work of the Salvationists was moving at a dizzying pace and there was no denying the problems of this crusading Army. The Booth home became "like a railway station," in Catherine's own words. But in sickness as in health Catherine Booth was still the Army Mother, and her bedroom was the conference room where many of the Army's expanding social policies were now argued and shaped. When not leading Army programs or spending time at his wife's bedside, William was working on his manuscript with Stead. It detailed William's plan to rescue the victims of vice and poverty through the establishment of refuges, workshops, and other establishments to be known as "The City Colony," "The Farm Colony," and "Overseas Colonies." William called it a "Scheme of Social Selection and Salvation."

The 140,000-word manuscript was finished on a Sunday morning in September 1890, an epic work that was, in Stead's words, to "echo round the world. I rejoice with an exceeding great joy," he concluded.

And from the sick woman on the bed came the barely audible words, "And I. . .and I most of all. Thank God. Thank God."

Even as she spoke, Catherine realized it was time for final good-byes. During her last weeks, Catherine's faith in all God's ways remained unshaken. "Don't be concerned about your dying," she said. "Only go on living well, and the dying will be all right."

William was racked by grief. Resolved to spend the last moments with her, he sent everyone from the room. Her hand rested in his, and he felt her release her thin gold wedding band from her finger and slip it on his own. "By this token we were united for time," she said, "and by it now we are united for eternity."

Surprising everyone, Catherine did not die. As her illness progressed over the next two years, many times the doctor said that her hours were numbered, and she believed it herself. Yet she rallied. From her sickbed she received dozens of visitors who came to say farewell. These conversations and her words of advice were written down. One author has stated that almost as important for the early Methodists as a life well lived was a death well died. Catherine's family and friends maintained constant bedside vigils.

She was unable to be present for The Salvation Army's twenty-fifth anniversary celebration in 1890 at the Crystal Palace. But she did send a message to those present. It was written in large letters on a sheet of calico coiled on a roller. As it was unwound, the audience read these words:

My Dear Children and Friends,

My place is empty, but my heart is with you. You are my joy and crown. Your battles, sufferings, and victories have been the chief interest of my life these past twenty-five years. They are so still. Go forward! Live holy lives. Be true to the Army. God is your strength. Love and seek the lost; bring them to the Blood. Make the people

*good; inspire them with the Spirit of Jesus Christ.
Love one another; help your comrades in dark
hours. I am dying under the Army Flag; it is
yours to live and fight under. God is my Salvation and Refuge in the storm. I send you my love
and blessing.*

—Catherine Booth

On Saturday afternoon, October 4, 1890, death came per-
ceptibly closer. No longer able to speak, Catherine pointed
to a text that hung above her children's photographs on a
mantle shelf: *My grace is sufficient for thee.* Someone
took it down and placed it near her on the bed, already
draped with the Army flag. Her family was there, comforting her and each other, singing some of her favorite
hymns. Each in turn tenderly kissed her. William Booth's
grey lion's mane of hair was swept back, as he bent low,
his lips on hers.

"Pa!" she cried, as his arms went round her. Then
she died.

The family was for a time inconsolable. Booth-Tucker,
one of her sons-in-law observed: "The anguish of bereave-
ment is the necessary penalty of love."

As news of Catherine Booth's death spread, telegrams,
letters, and words of condolence and praise poured into
the London headquarters of The Salvation Army. William
Booth wrote these words in *The War Cry:*

*The Army will mourn her loss and has rea-
sons for it; but she will live on, and on, and
on in the hearts and lives of thousands and
thousands of her daughters.*

177

William's good friend George Scott Railton was put in charge of funeral arrangements. Clapton Congress Hall, which seated five thousand, was used for the viewing. Over five days an estimated fifty thousand people—rich and poor alike—filed by the glass-covered casket to pay their final tribute.

Catherine's body was taken to the Olympia for the funeral service on October 13. The theater was a cavernous structure accommodating thirty-six thousand. Every seat was taken; countless people had to be turned away. *The War Cry* reported:

> *Slowly and sorrowfully, yet with an air of mingled hope and triumph, the advance guard of men and women officers filed their way, bearing the flags of various nations, together with those of some of the oldest corps presented in early days by Mrs. Booth. Others carried many-colored bannerettes. White badges on the left arm and white streamers from the flagpole took the place of customary crepe, and taught that they who mourned mourned not as those who had no hope; that heaven was a reality, and that they believed the Army Mother to be there.*
>
> *And when, borne on the shoulders of a band of officers, Mrs. Booth's mortal remains entered and passed slowly down the hall, preceded by her faithful nurse, who carried the flag under which she had breathed her last, few could restrain their tears, and it seemed as if a visible wave of sympathetic sorrow swept over the hearts of the entire audience.*[2]

The burial service on Tuesday morning, October 14, was memorable. The funeral march wound along the foggy Thames Embankment from Queen Victoria Street to Abney Park Cemetery, North London, a distance of about four miles. Three thousand Salvation Army officers marched with the Booth family in the procession. For the entire journey General William Booth stood upright in his carriage, bracing himself against the jolts and jars, conscious that people were craning to greet him, while he acknowledged their salutes.[3]

The burial at the cemetery had been limited to ten thousand persons. The coffin was placed on a platform and around it sat William, his children and grandchildren, and some officers. Commissioner Railton led the service at which William spoke these words:

My beloved Comrades and Friends:

You will readily understand that I find it a difficulty to talk to you this afternoon. To begin with, I could not be willing to talk without an attempt to make you hear, and sorrow doesn't feel like shouting.

Yet I cannot resist the opportunity of looking you in the face and blessing you in the name of the Lord, and in the name of our beloved one, who is looking down upon us, if she is not actually with us in this throng today.

As I have come riding through these, I suppose, hundreds of thousands of people this afternoon, who have bared their heads and who have blessed me in the name of the Lord at almost every revolution of the carriage wheels, my mind

*has been full of two feelings, which alternate—
one is uppermost one moment, and the other the
next—and yet which blend and amalgamate with
each other; and these are the feeling of sorrow
and the feeling of gratitude.*

*Those who know me—and I don't think I am
very difficult to understand—and those who
knew my darling, my beloved, will, I am sure,
understand how it is that my heart should be rent
with sorrow.*

William gave some analogies appropriate to these feelings of sorrow—that of a tree enjoyed for years that was then cut down; that of a faithful servant, a wise counselor, a friend, a mother who passed away:

*If you had had a wife, a sweet love of a wife,
who for forty years had never given you real
cause for grief; a wife who had stood with you
side by side in the battle's front, who had been a
comrade to you, ever willing to interpose herself
between you and the enemy and ever strongest
when the battle was fiercest, and your beloved
one had fallen before your eyes, I am sure there
would be some excuse for your sorrow!*

*Well, my comrades, you can roll all these
qualities into one personality and what would be
lost in each I have lost in all. There has been
taken away from me the delight of my eyes, the
inspiration of my soul, and we are about to lay
all that remains of her in the grave. I have
been looking right at the bottom of it here, and*

*calculating how soon they may bring and lay me
alongside of her, and my cry to God has been
that every remaining hour of my life may make
me readier to come and join her in death, to go
and embrace her in life in the Eternal City!*

*And yet, my comrades. . .my heart is full of
gratitude, too, that swells and makes me forget
my sorrow, that the long valley of the shadow of
death has been trodden, and that out of the dark
tunnel she has emerged into the light of day.
Death came to her with all his terrors, brandish-
ing his heart before her for two long years and
nine months. Again and again she went down to
the river's edge to receive his last thrust, as she
thought, but ever coming back to life again.
Thank God, she will see him [death] no more—
she is more than conqueror over the last enemy!*

*Death came to take her away from her loved
employment. She loved the fight! Her great sorrow to the last moment was: "I cannot be with
you when the clouds lower, when friends turn
and leave you, and sorrows come sweeping over
you; I shall no longer be there to put my arms
round you and cheer you on."*

*But she went away to help us! She promised
me many a time that what she could do for us in
the Eternal City should be done! The valley to
her was a dark one in having to tear her heart
away from so many whom she loved so well.
Again and again she said, "The roots of my
affections are very deep." But they had to be torn
up. One after another she gave us up; she made*

*the surrender with many loving words of coun-
sel, and left us to her Lord.*

*This afternoon my heart has been full of grati-
tude because her soul is now with Jesus. She
had a great capacity for suffering and a great
capacity for joy, and her heart is full of joy this
afternoon.*

*My heart has also been full of gratitude
because God lent me for so long a season such a
treasure. I have been thinking, if I had to point
out her three great qualities to you here, they
would be: First, she was good. She was washed
in the Blood of the Lamb. To the last moment
her cry was, "A sinner saved by grace." She was
a thorough hater of shams, hypocrisies, and
make-believes.*

*Second, she was love. Her whole soul was
full of tender, deep compassion. . . . Oh, how she
loved, how she compassioned, how she pitied the
suffering poor! How she longed to put her arms
round the sorrowful and help them!*

*Lastly, she was a warrior. She liked the fight.
She was not one who said to others, "Go!" but,
"Here, let me go!" And when there was the
necessity, she cried, "I will go." I never knew
her to flinch until her poor body compelled her
to lie aside.*

*Another thought fills my soul with praise—
that she has inspired so many to follow in her
track.*

*My comrades, I am going to meet her again.
I have never turned from her these forty years*

*for any journeyings on my mission of mercy, but
I have longed to get back, and have counted the
weeks, days, and hours which should take me
again to her side. When she has gone away from
me it has been just the same. And now she has
gone away for the last time. What, then, is there
left for me to do? Not to count the weeks, the
days, and the hours which shall bring me again
into her sweet company, seeing that I know not
what will be on the morrow, nor what an hour
may bring forth. My work plainly is to fill up the
weeks, the days, and the hours, and cheer my
poor heart as I go along with the thought that,
when I have served my Christ and my generation
according to the will of God—which I vow this
afternoon I will, to the last drop of my blood—
then I trust that she will bid me welcome to the
skies, as He bade her.*

God bless you all. Amen![4]

Night shadows were creeping over the graveyard as the
general knelt alongside his wife's coffin and imprinted
upon its lid a farewell kiss, while the tears of her children
and grandchildren fell silently.

eighteen

General William Booth survived his wife by twenty-two years. Her death after so long and painful an illness released his energies from a sad restraint, even though he was stunned by her loss. He threw himself into the vortex of comment swirling about him because of his newly published book *In Darkest England and The Way Out*. The work involved in establishing and defending his plans to help the poor was exhausting, so much so that it was decided to send him away from England on an extended international visit that included, among other places, Canada, the United States, Japan, Germany, South Africa, Australia, New Zealand, India, Denmark, Norway, Sweden, and Switzerland.

These travels, however, were not simply for recreation. He viewed the trip as an opportunity to fire the enthusiasm of the world for his new plan and, of course, to win souls. His family and Army officers, on the other hand, saw the trip as a change of pace that would enable Salvationists to meet the general and allow him to see firsthand what was happening outside England.

So early in 1891, a few months after Catherine's death, William began his world travels. These trips continued to the end of his life. Biographer Harold Begbie points out that William was no longer the outcast revivalist of Whitechapel, but the head of an international organization that had positioned itself to handle some of the most painful and troublesome social dangers and difficulties confronting civilization. With his flowing white hair and beard, William was easily recognizable, and his work was recognized in nearly every land as honestly inspired by love for humanity. After decades of faithful service, William was no longer an object of scorn; he had become a hero for the world.[1]

Wherever William toured, thousands came out to greet him and hear his words. In the winter of 1894–95, he made his second visit to the United States. A grand Jubilee Congress opened in New York on October 22, 1894, marking the beginning of William's coast-to-coast tour of the United States. He was sixty-five, always a tall, splendid-appearing man. He was well-received, and his tours were judged events of considerable importance.

Carnegie Hall was filled for William's first public appearance. He spoke of *In Darkest England* and the plan it proposed. "It isn't wicked to be reduced to rags," William stated. "It is not a sin to starve, to pawn the few sticks of furniture to buy food and pay the rent. It is a misfortune that comes to people, honest and good people, in hard times or when work is hard to get. It is such people that the social scheme means to help."

The book described in dreadful detail the social evils of the day—one of its major purposes was to shock the respectable middle class out of its complacency. But not only did William show the magnitude of the problem, he offered *a way out.* The industrial (City Colonies) shelters and homes would give immediate relief to the destitute; the Farm Colonies would provide temporary employment that could develop into more permanency; and emigration (Overseas Colonies) would provide a permanent home in countries less crowded such as Canada, Australia, and South Africa. In the Carnegie Hall audience listening to William sat many of America's wealthiest men and women whose hearts were touched by the dignified bearing and unforgettable oratory of the general.

"The Salvation Army has the machinery for carrying out such a plan—in fact, we are already at work on it," he pointed out. "But the scale on which it could operate depends on public support." He dramatized this point by using the illustration of a London cab horse. "When the horse falls down, it is helped up, given shelter for the night, food for its stomach, and, finally, work is allotted by which it can earn its grain. This is the essence of *the way out*—to help people to their feet, to supply shelter, food, and work."

After a similar address in Cambridge, Professor Charles Norton, of Harvard, compared William to St. Bernard at the time of the first crusade. Prime ministers, governors, cabinet members, senators and congressmen, paupers and millionaires, the ignorant and the educated, clergymen and sinners, all listened to William's pleas for the unfortunate. The Army's social welfare program grew rapidly as a result of this tour. His 18,453-mile itinerary in Canada and the United States, with addresses in eighty-six cities where he spoke at 340 meetings, attracted 437,000 people. Thousands came forward to the penitent form. During the twenty-four-week tour, the general spent 847 hours on trains. And that was just one tour. This type of travel was to mark his work for the rest of his life.

In 1902, William made his fourth visit to the United States to inspect the Army's work and, in particular, the Farm Colonies that had been started. He saw twentieth-century America on this trip. Once more he was given a triumphant American welcome—nearly two thousand people sailed down the bay in a flotilla of eleven tugs and two sidewheel steamers to meet his ship at quarantine. The vessels were decorated with streamers reading, "Welcome General," and on each of the tugs a Salvation Army band played. After a twenty-one-gun salute and seventy-three bombs—one for each year of William's life—the flotilla escorted the *Philadelphia* to her dock. Upon disembarking, William faced a battery of reporters and photographers and told of his plans. Reporting back to his London headquarters, William wrote, "It was a day of days, one of the most remarkable of my life."[2]

But the general's last years were also touched with sorrow. The year after William's fourth tour of the United States, his daughter Emma Booth-Tucker was in a tragic train accident during her return from an inspection trip to a place called Amity Colony in Colorado. On October 28, 1903, at Dean Lake, Missouri, the train ran into an open switch, the cars were wrecked, and forty-three-year-old Emma was the only fatality. Her husband, Commander Frederick Booth-Tucker, was distraught and barely able to struggle through the several mass memorial meetings and the enormous public funeral held at the national headquarters of The Salvation Army in New York. Emma also left behind six children, including three-year-old Muriel, who years later was to become a colonel and head the Army's work in Ireland.

William's son-in-law, Commissioner Booth-Tucker, was devastated by the loss of his wife. His work in the United States came to an end. Soon after Emma's death, he again consecrated himself to the great work of The Salvation Army in India, where he and Emma had begun their ministry.

"Over fifty million men and women are racked by physical and spiritual starvation," the commissioner explained to his father-in-law. "It is where I belong."

"Get into their skins, Tucker," William said to his son-in-law, whose work there is now legendary.[3]

William, himself, was grief-stricken over the loss of his much-loved daughter. Not only had Emma helped the family in innumerable ways when she was young, but she had also returned to London to be with her mother during the last months of Catherine's illness. As he had so many times in his life, William grieved privately but continued his public work.

In 1907, he paid two visits to the United States, one a stopover on his way to Japan where the emperor received him. Twenty-five thousand people gathered to see the seventy-eight-year-old general, breaking all records. When he returned to England, William received an honorary doctorate of civil law from Oxford before he set sail again for America—his sixth and last visit. This trip was plagued by illness. William still had a young mind and spirit, but his physical body was weakened from thousands of miles of continuous travel and constant meetings and speeches. The ocean trip on the *Virginian* was a pleasant one, with Guglielmo Marconi (inventor of the wireless) as a fellow passenger and interested visitor to William's shipboard lectures.

William's itinerary included visiting the principal cities of the East and Midwest. In Washington, President and Mrs. Theodore Roosevelt held a luncheon for him and his daughter Evangeline. The general told the president about his trip to Japan and about the work of The Salvation Army worldwide. John Wanamaker, one of the Army's staunchest friends and supporters, was chairman of William's meetings in Philadelphia.

But as the general met with emperors, presidents, famous statesmen, and educators, he always thought of the value of these contacts to the work of The Salvation Army and of how their influence could be translated into tangible aid for the unfortunate and downtrodden. In all the countries he visited, William Booth was asked by kings, governors, and politicians what he would recommend they do for the alleviation of human suffering and the removal of poverty. He had become an authority, but more than anything the general wanted these powerful men of influence to understand, as he often told his Army officers, "You cannot make a man clean [simply] by washing his shirt."

Wherever he went, reporters clamored for an interview. In New York City, William was so weak that several times during the interview he was forced to put his head down on the table to regain his strength. One reporter wrote, "Feeble as he is, that little spark in his eye that electrifies anyone he looks at tells the secret of his endurance—he is a human live wire perpetually charged from an inexhaustible storage battery of nervous energy."

William Booth was empowered by the Holy Spirit. But the eyes and the nervous energy were waning. On November 9, 1907, accompanied by his daughter Evangeline, the general sailed from New York. The band played "God Be with You till We Meet Again" as the general bade farewell to America for the last time.

Soon after his trip to America, William's sight began to fail. Still, as he was able, he traveled throughout England and the Continent, conducting large and small meetings and speaking to convicts in prisons.

On his eighty-third birthday, William was able to enjoy a huge celebration in his honor. In May 1912, he addressed ten thousand people in Albert Hall, his last public appearance, and announced, "I am going into dry dock for repairs." They heard the bent and nearly blind old man declare: "While women weep as they do now, I'll fight; while little children go hungry as they do now, I'll fight; while men go to prison, in and out, in and out, I'll fight; while there is a poor lost girl upon the streets, I'll fight; where there yet remains one dark soul without the light of God, I'll fight—I'll fight to the very end."

William was game to the very last. An operation in 1910 left him sightless in his right eye. The fearless old warrior said to the surgeon after they removed the bandages, "I see no light. I am blind. . . . Doctor, God has helped me through many a storm and He will help me through this."

His left eye was not yet totally blind, but his sight was greatly diminished by what was thought to be a cataract.

Then in late May 1912, an operation on the left eye resulted in complications that left him totally blind. His son Bramwell was at his bedside. William took his son's hand. "I shall never see your face again?" were his first words. Then, after a moment, he added resolutely, "God must know best. Bramwell, I have done what I could for God and the people with my eyes. Now I shall see what I can do for God and the people without my eyes."

Even though he was sightless, the old general's eyes were fixed on those who so desperately needed help. The problem of the homeless obsessed him. "I want you to do more for the homeless of the world, the homeless men," he urged his son. "Mind, I'm not thinking of this country only, but of *all* lands."

"Yes, General," Bramwell promised. "I understand."

"The homeless women—ah, my boy, we don't know what it means to be without a home."

"Yes, General, I follow."

"And the homeless children, Bramwell, look after the homeless. Promise me."

And Bramwell promised. But Booth, even in sickness, managed to draw on his sense of humor: "Mind—if you don't I shall come back and haunt you!"

The old soldier fought valiantly for his life for three more days, even though he longed for a rest. Finally at 10:13 P.M., August 20, 1912, William Booth went to be with his Lord. In the words of poet Nicholas Vachel Lindsay:

Christ came gently with a robe and crown
For Booth the soldier, while the throng knelt down.
He saw King Jesus. They were face-to-face,
*   And he knelt a-weeping in that holy place.*

191

nineteen

A t 9:00 A.M., August 21, 1912, staff officers arriving at International Headquarters were stunned to read this simple message in the window: "The General Has Laid Down His Sword."

News of General Booth's death was flashed around the world. Grief of a most close and personal character burst from the heart of the world. They mourned this godly man. Biographer Begbie pointed out, "No man ever finished his earth's battle with so universal a triumph. . . . It was not merely that every newspaper of any consequence throughout the whole civilized world paid its tribute of admiration and respect to the dead warrior; it was not that messages of sympathy from the great people of the earth rained in from every quarter of the globe; these things spoke for much; these things witnessed to the respect of respectability for one who had been in his middle-life the most assailed, ridiculed, and persecuted of men; but what attested more than anything else to the triumph of his life was the individual sorrow of the poorest and the lowliest in every country throughout the world."[1]

The *New York Tribune* wrote: "In the list of those who have unselfishly devoted their entire lives to the uplifting of humanity, no name stands higher than that of General William Booth. . . . His field of labor was the world, and the peoples of every race and clime had opportunity to hear the message of hope and promise he so effectively preached to the downtrodden and unfortunate." President Taft sent a message of tribute and condolence. Other officials of church and state sent messages, including the German emperor, England's King George V, the prime minister, and the archbishop of Canterbury.

An enormous outpouring of tributes to the general appeared in newspapers and magazines throughout the world. The *Daily Chronicle* (London, August 21, 1912) proclaimed:

Today we have the mournful duty of chronicling the passing of William Booth, the Head of that vast Organization, The Salvation Army. The world has lost its greatest missionary evangelist, one of the supermen of the age. Almost every land on the face of the globe knows this pioneer and his Army, the Army which has waged such long, determined, and successful battle against the world's ramparts of sin and woe. Not one country, but fifty, will feel today a severe personal loss. From Lapland to Honolulu heads will be bowed in sorrow at the news that that striking figure who has been responsible for so much of the religious progress of the world of today is no more.

The stupendous crusade which he initiated had the very humblest beginnings. It opened in the slummy purlieus of Nottingham, that city which gave to the world two of the greatest religious leaders of modern times—General Booth and Dr. Paton. It has passed through periods of open enmity, opposition, criticism, but its Leader and his band of devoted helpers have never lost sight of their high aim. They were engaged in "war on the hosts that keep the underworld submerged," and they have now long been justified by their unparalleled achievements. The time of scorn and indifference passed, and General Booth lived to receive honor at the hands of kings and princes, and to have their support for his work.

It is not given to every man who sets out with a great purpose to accomplish his aim. But of General Booth it may be said that he did more. His Movement reached dimensions of which he probably never dreamed in its early days, yet the extraordinary results made him ever hungrier for conquest. In a way the latter years of his life were perhaps the most notable of his whole career. He displayed a vitality and enthusiasm which seemed to increase with the weight of time. At a time when most men seek a greater measure of repose, General Booth worked on with all the freshness of early years. And it can be said that he died in harness. He did not lift his finger from the pulse of the far-reaching Organization which he brought into being until death called.

The story of the growth of The Salvation Army is the most remarkable in the history of the work of the spiritual, social, and material regeneration of the submerged. From the byways of all the world human derelicts, which other agencies passed by, have been rescued. No one was too degraded, too repulsive to be neglected. The work is too great to be estimated in a way which can show its extent. It has been achieved mainly by two great factors. The first is perfect organization. Lord Wolseley once described General Booth as the greatest organizer in the world. The second feature was the wonderful personality of the Army's chief. He impressed it not only upon his colleagues but upon those whom he wished to rescue, and on the public at large. He radiated human sympathy and enthusiasm. His loss will be a heavy one for the world; it will be a severe blow for the Army. But we cannot think that his good work has not been built upon sound foundations, and that the war he directed so ably and so long will be relaxed. Nationally the Army has done magnificent work in fifty countries, and it has, therefore, tended to promote a greater spirit of brotherhood among the nations. Today the whole world will unite to pay its tribute to a splendid life of devotion to a great cause. To that world he leaves a splendid example, and it will be the highest tribute that can be paid to his memory to keep green that lofty example which he set before all peoples.[2]

195

For three days William's body lay in state at Clapton's Congress Hall where 150,000 people filed past the old warrior's casket. On August 27, he was borne to Olympia, the vast exhibition hall on Hammersmith Road, West London, and forty thousand people flocked to the funeral service. Officers on furlough from all over the world—among them the general's daughter, Commissioner Evangeline from New York—knelt beside the casket to rededicate themselves to God and the Army. Along with them knelt thieves, tramps, prostitutes, and the lost and outcasts to whom Booth had given his heart.

Almost unrecognized in that audience sat Britain's Queen Mary, a staunch admirer of William Booth, along with her Lord Chamberlain and Lord Shaftesbury. (The queen had elected to come at the last moment, without warning.) She sat alongside a somewhat shabby woman. Shyly the woman confided to the queen that once she had been a prostitute and only the Salvationists had saved her from death. She then described to the queen how later, at a meeting with General Booth, he had heard her story and said to her, "My girl, when you get to heaven, you'll have a place of honor, because Mary Magdalene will give you one of the best places."

The queen was very interested in the woman's story. Then the woman said, "You see the three red carnations on the casket? I came early to get an aisle seat, and when the casket passed, I placed the flowers on the lid. You see, he cared for the likes of us."

The next day the funeral procession, solemn yet triumphal, was led by banners of white—palms of victory—the casket borne on a bier drawn by two chestnut horses. Forty bands played the death march from Handel's *Saul*.

Ten thousand uniformed Salvationists fell into step behind the bier. The size of the crowds packing the line to the Abney Park Cemetery in Stoke Newington could not be estimated. They packed the streets and sidewalks in an unending mass. People leaned out of windows, and even the housetops were crowded. City offices were closed and shuttered; flags of all nations hung at half-mast. Around William's grave lay wreaths from the king and queen of England, from Queen Alexandra, from Kaiser Wilhelm of Germany, and from the American ambassador.

As the funeral procession neared its end, the international staff band struck up a new song, and a gasp ran through the crowd. The tune was known to all:

Home, home, sweet, sweet, home,
  There's no friend like Jesus,
There's no place like home.

Tears filled everyone's eyes. The meaning of that well-loved melody struck a responsive chord in their hearts.

At the graveside stood Bramwell Booth on whom the reins of the Army had fallen. "I loved him, and you loved him, and he was our leader. He led us and we are going to follow him," Bramwell said simply.

London's *Punch* declared:

No Laurelled blazon rests above his bier,
Yet a great people bows its stricken head
Where he who fought without reproach or fear
Soldier of Christ, lies dead.[3]

197

epilogue

I t didn't come as a surprise to anyone that the general's eldest son, William Bramwell Booth, should succeed his father as The Salvation Army's second general. The day following William's death, a document written and sealed in an envelope twenty-two years earlier was opened and Bramwell's name, as successor, was read. Bramwell, who had been chief of staff for so many years and who had devoted his life to the Christian Mission and The Salvation Army since he was sixteen, was now fifty-six years old.

It was, in fact, Bramwell, gifted with a legal mind, who was always the able administrator, helping to carry forward his father's ideals and keep the movement expanding. Bramwell Booth could never have founded a Salvation Army, but it is also highly probable that William Booth could not have built as efficient an organization without the giftedness of his son.

General Bramwell Booth served in that capacity until April 12, 1928, when ill health forced him to seek treatment and led to his being asked to resign on January 8, 1929. This eventually led to a reform of the basic government of The Salvation Army. Principles involved were more important than personalities, and the principle of electing a general prevented the establishment of a Booth dynasty and enabled the Army to utilize its finest available talent as leaders.

Bramwell Booth was succeeded by Edward J. Higgins, chief of staff, who served as general until 1934 when he retired at age seventy. Commander Evangelinc Booth was a leading candidate to take General Higgins's place, which she did in November 1934, relinquishing her command in the United States. She had already completed thirty years of service in the states when she sailed for London on November 23, 1934, to assume the duties of the highest office in The Salvation Army. She was the third and last of the Booths to receive the generalship.

Evangeline Booth had been in the forefront of the reform movement, as were the highest Salvation Army officers in England and in other countries, believing as they all did that it was in the best interest of the Army that a more democratic process be set in motion to appoint top administrative positions. Since 1930, the ministry of The Salvation Army throughout the world has become increasingly effective under a series of able international leaders.

The story of the work of The Salvation Army in World Wars I and II, and its worldwide humanitarian relief efforts would require another book. The basic social services developed by William and Catherine Booth have remained a visible expression of the Army's strong religious principles. New programs that address contemporary needs have been added. Among these are disaster relief services, day care centers, summer camps, holiday assistance, services for senior citizens, hospitals and medical facilities, shelters for battered wives and children, family and career counseling, vocational training, correctional services, and drug rehabilitation.

Today the operations of The Salvation Army worldwide are supervised by trained, commissioned officers. They proclaim the gospel and serve as administrators, teachers, social workers, counselors, youth leaders, and musicians.

Candidates for officership undergo an intensive two-year course in residence at Salvation Army schools for officers' training. The curriculum combines theory and field practice. This includes Salvation Army doctrine and regulations, sociology and social work, psychology, homiletics, public speaking, Bible studies, church history, community relations, business administration, and more.

At graduation, cadets are ordained as ministers, commissioned as lieutenants, and assigned to active duty while continuing their education. Lieutenants are required to devote five years to additional studies.

Promotion is based on length of service, character, efficiency, devotion to duty, and capacity for increased responsibility. The ranks in The Salvation Army are lieutenant, captain, major, lieutenant colonel, colonel, and commissioner. The international leader holds the rank of general and is selected by a high council of active duty commissioners and territorial commanders.

Salvation Army officers must devote full-time to Army work. An officer who marries must marry another Salvation Army officer or leave his or her officer status. Husband and wife hold equal rank and perform assigned duties. As ordained ministers of the gospel, they are authorized to perform pastoral services for their congregation, marriage ceremonies, funeral services, and infant dedications. They also provide counseling and consolation to the bereaved.

The outreach of The Salvation Army has been expanded to include 103 countries, and the gospel is faithfully preached by its officers and soldiers in 160 languages.

Dr. Wilbur Chapman had an interview with General William Booth on one of his last visits to the United States which led to these observations:

When I looked into his face and saw him brush back his hair from his brow, and heard him speak of the trials and conflicts and the victories, I said: "General Booth, tell me what has been the secret of your success all the way through."

He hesitated a second, and I saw the tears come into his eyes and steal down his cheeks, and then he said: "I will tell you the secret. God has had all there was of me. There have been men with greater opportunities; but from the day I got the poor of London on my heart, and a vision of what Jesus Christ could do with the poor of London, I made up my mind that God would have all of William Booth there was. And if there is anything of power in The Salvation Army today, it is because God has all the adoration of my heart, all the power of my will, and all the influence of my life."

He looked at me a minute, and I soon learned another secret of his power. He said, "When do you go?" I said, "In five minutes." He said, "Pray"; and I dropped on my knees, with General Booth by my side, and prayed a

*stammering and stuttering prayer. Then he talked
with God about the outcasts of London, the poor
of New York, the lost of China, the great world
lying in wickedness. He opened his eyes as if he
were looking into the very face of Jesus, and
with sobs he prayed God's blessing upon every
mission worker, every evangelist, every minister,
every Christian. With his eyes still overflowing
with tears, he bade me goodbye, and started
away, past eighty years of age, to preach on the
continent. And I learned from William Booth that
the greatness of a man's power is the measure of
his surrender. It is not a question of who you are
or of what you are, but of whether God controls
you.[1]*

Paul A. Rader, current general of The Salvation Army,
writing in *New Frontier* (May 7, 1998), the West's territorial newspaper, reminded readers of Isaiah 58:6–12,
sometimes referred to as The Salvation Army Charter. It
was a favorite of General William Booth. "It has a very
contemporary ring!" General Rader wrote. "It calls us to
be personally involved in acting responsibly and com-
passionately toward the imprisoned, the homeless, the
poor, the hungry, the inadequately clothed. When Jesus
speaks of our giving an account before Him in Matthew
25, He speaks to the same social issues. And He assures us
that what we do for those in the most desperate situations
of poverty, abuse, loneliness, and neglect is done for Him.

"The Salvation Army has a global reputation for its
timely and efficient response to major disasters. We have
mounted extensive programs of assistance to refugees and
those caught up in complex humanitarian emergencies in

places like Rwanda and Bosnia. Our response to recent disasters in the USA that have taken such a tragic toll of human life and resulted in such widespread destruction of property have given the Army an unprecedented profile as a major provider of disaster and emergency services. But Salvationists are called to be more than compassion by proxy. From the passionate plea of the prophet Isaiah to the haunting challenge of our Lord Jesus in Matthew 25, the gospel calls us to be personally involved—hands-on. Every Salvationist should be personally engaged in some form of service to others. It is a vital dimension of the living out of the gospel we preach in a world of suffering, neglect, violence, and need. What are you doing to care for Jesus' sake?[2]

"Is this not the fast that I have chosen:
To loose the bonds of wickedness,
To undo the heavy burdens,
To let the oppressed go free,
And that you break every yoke?
Is it not to share your bread with the hungry,
And that you bring to your house the poor who
*   are cast out;*
When you see the naked, that you cover him,
And not hide yourself from your own flesh?
Then your light shall break forth like the
*   morning,*
Your healing shall spring forth speedily,
And your righteousness shall go before you;
The glory of the LORD shall be your rear guard.
Then you shall call, and the LORD will answer;
You shall cry, and He will say,
'Here I am.'

If you take away the yoke from your midst,
The pointing of the finger, and speaking
   wickedness,
If you extend your soul to the hungry
And satisfy the afflicted soul,
Then your light shall dawn in the darkness,
And your darkness shall be as the noonday.
The LORD will guide you continually,
And satisfy your soul in drought,
And strengthen your bones;
You shall be like a watered garden,
And like a spring of water, whose waters do
   not fail.
Those from among you
Shall build the old waste places;
You shall raise up the foundations of many
   generations;
And you shall be called the Repairer of the
   Breach,
The Restorer of Streets to Dwell In."

ISAIAH 58:6–12 NKJV

Notes

Chapter One

1. Roger J. Green, *Catherine Booth: A Biography of the Cofounder of The Salvation Army* (Grand Rapids, Mich.: Baker Books, 1996), 95.
2. Ibid., 97.
3. Ibid., 108.
4. Ibid., 107.

Chapter Two

1. George S. Railton, General Booth (London: Salvationist Publishing and Supplies, 1912), 5.
2. Ibid., 5–6.
3. Ibid., 11.
4. Ibid., 16.
5. Ibid., 19–20.
6. Ibid., 29.

Chapter Three

1. Green, 43.
2. Railton, 30–31.
3. Harold Begbie, *The Life of General William Booth,* vol. 1 (New York: Macmillan, 1920), 125–26.
4. Green, 26–27.
5. Ibid., 31.
6. Ibid., 36–37.
7. Booth Papers, Mss. 64799.

Chapter Four

1. Railton, 42–43.
2. Catherine Booth, *The Highway of Our God* (Atlanta: The Salvation Army, 1986), 74–76.

Chapter Five

1. Green, 72.
2. Ibid., 70.
3. Booth Papers, Mss. 64803.
4. Green, 73.
5. Franklin De L. Booth-Tucker, *The Life of Catherine Booth,* vol. 1 (London: Simpkin, Marshall, Hamilton, Kent & Co., 1912), 247.
6. Green, 85.
7. Ibid.
8. Bramwell Booth, *Echoes and Memories* (London: Hodder and Stoughton, 1925), 7.
9. Catherine Booth, *Practical Religion* (Atlanta: The Salvation Army, 1986), 11–12.

Chapter Six

1. Robert Randall, *The Story of The Salvation Army,* vol. 1 (London: Thomas Nelson & Sons, 1947), 248.
2. Ibid.

3. St. John Ervine, *God's Soldier: General William Booth* (New York: Polygraphic Co. of America, 1925), 251–52.
4. Ibid., 252.
5. Booth Papers, Mss. 64805.
6. Green, 141.
7. Ervine, 259.
8. Randall, 17–18.
9. Ervine, 1:11.
10. Ervine, 1:277; Booth-Tucker, *The Life of Catherine Booth,* 1:547.
11. Green, 155.

Chapter Seven
1. Richard Collier, *The General Next to God* (St. James Place, London: Collins, 1965), 26.

Chapter Nine
1. Robert Sandall, *The History of The Salvation Army,* vol. 1 (London: Nelson & Hodder & Stoughton, 1947–86), 46–48.

Chapter Ten
1. Sandall, *The History of The Salvation Army,* 1:48.
2. Collier, 52.
3. Sandall, 34.

Chapter Eleven
1. Sandall, 1:54–55.
2. Ibid., 35.
3. Norma H. Murdoch, *Origins of The Salvation Army* (Knoxville, Tenn.: Univ. of Tenn. Press, 1994), 50–51.
4. Ibid., 51.

Chapter Twelve
1. Green, 164.
2. Collier, 62–64.
3. Herbert A. Wiseby Jr., *Soldiers Without Swords* (New York: The Macmillan Co., 1955), 18–19.
4. Information on this account was taken from Richard Collier's *The General Next to God* (pp. 64–66) and Robert Sandall's *The History of The Salvation Army,* vol. 1 (pp. 229–30).
5. The information on this War Congress was essentially gleaned from Robert Sandall's book *The History of The Salvation Army,* vol. 1, chapter 19. This account written by Thomas B. Coombs was found on page 236 of Sandall's book.

Chapter Thirteen
1. Taken from The Salvation Army USA website at http://www.salvation-armyusa./org/home.htm
2. Harry Edward Neal, *The Hallelujah Army* (Philadelphia & New York: Chilton & Co., 1961).
3. Some of the material in this chapter was gleaned from Herbert A. Wisbey Jr.'s book *Soldiers Without Swords*.

Chapter Fourteen
1. Sandall, 1:217.
2. Information found in Herbert A. Wisbey Jr.'s book *Soldiers Without Swords*, p. 12. The account of the work of the Shirleys is based on articles written by Eliza Shirley at different times and published in *The War Cry*. The first was on July 9, 1881. The second, entitled "Pioneering the Work in the United States," was printed in serial form in the issues of November 28 and December 5, 1908. The third was entitled "Born in American Stable" and appeared in serial form in the September 12, 19, 26, and October 3, 1925 issues. Mrs. Commandant Eliza (Shirley) Symmonds lived to be seventy and died on September 18, 1932 in Racine, Wisconsin.

Chapter Sixteen
1. Booth-Tucker, *The Life of Catherine Booth,* vol. 2 (London: Simpkin, Marshall, Hamilton, Kent & Co., 1912), 185.
2. Ibid., 2:198.
3. Bramwell Booth, 373.
4. Ibid., 248.
5. Booth-Tucker, 2:295–96.
6. Edward H. McKinley, *Marching to Glory: The History of The Salvation Army in the United States* (San Francisco: Harper & Row, 1980), 94–95.

Chapter Seventeen
1. Green, 194–95.
2. Booth-Tucker, 2:656–57.
3. Collier, 190.
4. Booth-Tucker, 2:413–17.

Chapter Eighteen
1. Harold Begbie, *William Booth, Founder of The Salvation Army,* vol. 2. Information in these paragraphs excerpted from Begbie's book in the chapter entitled "At the Threshhold of a New Phase."
2. Wiseby, 135.
3. McKinley, 93.

Chapter Nineteen
1. Begbie, 318.
2. George S. Railton, *The Authoritative Life of General William Booth, Founder of The Salvation Army* (New York: The Reliance Trading Co., 1912), 253–55.
3. Information for this chapter gleaned from the many books used throughout the writing of this book, but in this chapter primarily from Herbert A. Wisbey's fine work *Soldiers Without Swords,* and Richard Collier's equally fine work, *The General Next to God.*

Epilogue
1. Charles T. Bateman, *Life of General Booth* (New York, London: Association Press, 1912), 93–95.
2. Used by permission.

HEROES OF THE FAITH

This exciting biographical series explores the lives of famous Christian men and women throughout the ages. These trade paper books will inspire and encourage you to follow the example of these "Heroes of the Faith" who made Christ the center of their existence. 208 pages each. Only $3.97 each!

Gladys Aylward,
Missionary to China
Sam Wellman

•

John Bunyan,
Author of The Pilgrim's Progress
Sam Wellman

•

William Carey, Father of Missions
Sam Wellman

•

Amy Carmichael
Abandoned to God
Sam Wellman

•

George Washington Carver,
Inventor and Naturalist
Sam Wellman

•

Fanny Crosby, the Hymn Writer
Bernard Ruffin

•

Jim Elliot, Missionary to Ecuador
Susan Miller

•

Billy Graham, the Great Evangelist
Sam Wellman

•

C.S. Lewis,
Author of Mere Christianity
Sam Wellman

•

David Livingstone,
Missionary and Explorer
Sam Wellman

•

Martin Luther, the Great Reformer
Dan Harmon

D.L. Moody,
the American Evangelist
Bonnie Harvey

•

Samuel Morris,
the Apostle of Simple Faith
W. Terry Whalin

•

Mother Teresa,
Missionary of Charity
Sam Wellman

•

George Müller, Man of Faith
Bonnie Harvey

•

Watchman Nee, Man of Suffering
Bob Laurent

•

John Newton,
Author of "Amazing Grace"
Anne Sandberg

•

Mary Slessor, Queen of Calabar
Sam Wellman

•

Charles Spurgeon,
the Great Orator
Dan Harmon

•

Corrie ten Boom, Heroine of Haarlem
Sam Wellman

•

Sojourner Truth,
American Abolitionist
W. Terry Whalin

•

John Wesley, the Great Methodist
Sam Wellman

Available wherever books are sold.
Or order from:
Barbour Publishing, Inc.
P.O. Box 719
Uhrichsville, Ohio 44683
http://www.barbourbooks.com

If you order by mail, add $2.00 to your order for shipping.
Prices subject to change without notice.